PIER PAGANO

NO ONE CAN TELL YOU WHO YOU ARE EXCEPT YOU

A Simple Guide To Knowing Your True Self

No One Can Tell You Who You Are Except You:
A Simple Guide To Knowing Your True Self
©2021, Pier Pagano

ISBN: 978-1-09836-699-5
ISBN eBook: 978-1-09836-700-8

Epigraph

To love oneself is the beginning of a lifelong romance

—Oscar Wilde

Introduction

Welcome to the Life Essence Tribe! Your original blueprint is the pathway that determines your choices. Its gift is in teaching you how to embrace or reject the old patterns you grew up with. Every one of your life experiences from the moment you came into the world is a part of your blueprint.

Every word that you've ever spoken or has been spoken to you by parents, friends, teachers, even strangers, has shaped the way you view yourself and the world. Once you have examined each hurt or victory, you are free to write your own blueprint. You will not need to keep them all, because some no longer serve you. Others may have never served you. At this point, your unique experiences allow you to be the person you have nurtured and cared for. You are the only you. Every part of you is necessary and worth loving. Life is an adventure and you are an explorer. You have arrived here because of the twists and turns along your way.

I created a program called Repattern to help overcome the negativity and fears that hold you back from fulfilling your potential and experiencing joy. In order to shift the blockages and encumbrances in your life and create changes, you need to honestly examine your patterns. If you're willing to do the work, you can overcome anything. Join me on this explorative journey into your internal closet. Learning to love yourself is the beginning of a lifelong relationship and opens the door to healthy relationships with others.

Dear Diary, How Do I Know My Purpose?/Listen To Your Heart

This is actually a very good question.

Answer: It's not something you need to search for.

Once you learn to accept every part of yourself as necessary and welcome, you know who you are and your purpose becomes clear. You don't need to look for it because it's been within you since the moment you were born. It will become plain to you as soon as you're ready to move forward into your authentic self. Maybe my own experience will resonate with you.

As a child, I had a lot of unchanneled emotions and feelings. Although no one was interested in listening to me, I still had a lot to say. So, I wrote them in my diary. In the 1960s, journals were called diaries. Every young girl had one, heart-shaped lock and tiny key included. This book held our deepest teenage secrets about boys we liked as well as our hopes and wishes. Every night we faithfully wrote, then locked and tucked our tome under the pillow before falling asleep. After high school, my diary turned into a hardcover notebook with sewn in pages. I recorded my dreams, hopes and wishes, but now I included my questions for the universe. I had quite a few. At that time I was living in a rented room, working several jobs and finishing my last year of high school. I didn't completely understand why my life was so different from that of my friends, but I did know that home wasn't a safe place, so I left.

My unanswered questions turned into paragraphs-obsessive rumi-nations on how to achieve a more connected and satisfying life than the one I was born into. Educating myself by reading many different philosophies only emphasized what had already become increasingly clear: I would need to figure out who I was before anyone else could tell me who to be. I started writing my thoughts differently; now it became a daily blog about the things that disturbed me and the things that intrigued me. I began talking to people and hearing their stories too. I found that releasing my thoughts and connecting with others helped me to discover my true self. I am not alone. The people who respond to me and contribute to my growth are the same people I help. Our tribe believes that no one can tell you who you are when you know who you are. It is proof that your purpose will find you when you're ready.Welcome to the most satisfying relationship you can possibly have- the one with yourself. You are enough.

Loving yourself is not the same as rewarding yourself in a material way. Pleasures like shopping sprees or vacations are enjoyable, but they obstruct real contact with your heart. Inside everyone is a wounded child that needs healing. As adults, we continue our old blueprint unless we address it. Jealousy stems from fear of abandonment; abuse causes shame, repetition or dysfunction. All of these negative patterns inflict loss of ego and self-worth and hold us back from wholeness. In order to move forward, we need to find the courage within to confront the painful memories we carry. While fear of consequences thwarts the power to evolve, guidance and intuition promote the search for the whole self. Embracing your ability to forgive is a release from the emotional and physical wounds that have impacted you. Every single experience you have comes with the gift of knowledge. No matter how painful, it always strengthens your empowerment in a positive way.

Start by asking yourself these five questions.

What do I like?

What do I love?

What makes me happy?

What are my strengths?

What are my weaknesses?

Listening to your heart is a necessary tool for growth.

I Know Who I Am/Connecting With Your Best Friend

Do we see ourselves as others see us? Or do we define ourselves by how others see us?

Everything you don't like about yourself can be an asset once you figure out how much to amplify or quiet it to turn any situation around positively. Viewing a "negative" behavior differently works to serve you by changing your impact on everyone in your life. Repressing any of the qualities you don't see as attractive causes confusion and loathing within yourself. It's up to you to honestly weigh each and every one of your traits to see how important it is in enhancing your strengths. When you understand how your future is mapped by past and present choices, it becomes second nature to accept that your many inner personalities are all useful and here to serve you.

Embracing yourself and claiming your value is integral to a compassionate and lifelong relationship with yourself. It is essential to start the quest with self-love and patience. Confidence radiates from within when you enjoy your own company. Other people will be attracted to your energy. Shedding layers and judgements you have collected along the way is a sometimes painful process but worth the work. Being authentically you is definitely a road with detours. It may be confusing in the moment, but every twist and turn leads somewhere you need to go, even if you don't yet know where that is. Living your best life is knowing and owning who you are. It's not surprising that others like you. After all, you're amazing.

I think some of us may have forgotten how much fun it is to be by ourselves, especially with the world so upended at this time. It's absolutely possible to still feel lonely, even when you're surrounded with the virtual ability to connect anywhere, anytime with another human. The pervasive fears of ending up alone can make us hold on to the wrong people because we'd rather have them than no one. It can cause anxiety and delusive concerns. We feel incomplete as if something is missing when we're not sharing our lives with another person. Once panic sets in, we're scrambling. Bad friends, abusive partners, anyone, come on down. Please. We don't want to be alone with ourselves. But why not? I'm about to tell you.

Choosing a toxic relationship is not an acceptable alternative to being on your own. Enjoying yourself by yourself and avoiding energy drainers seem preferable to me. If you don't think so, it's time to take inventory of your choices. Going from one relationship to another without stopping is a way of trying to leave the mess behind. You're moving on, yay! Not yay. You are the mess. And you're coming with you. The relationship you have with yourself is the one that's going to last until you die. The way you treat yourself is the way you'll allow others to treat you. Have compassion for yourself because it will teach the world how to behave toward you. When you treat yourself with kindness and love, you send out a message that attracts a like-minded tribe of others who recognize and thrive on positive energy. Because you're no longer willing to accept people who tell you who you are or how to be, you stop trying to please others. Own what is holding you back and educate yourself to accept that you are worth loving and project it forward. You deserve better. You deserve to be healthy. The only caveat is that you believe it.

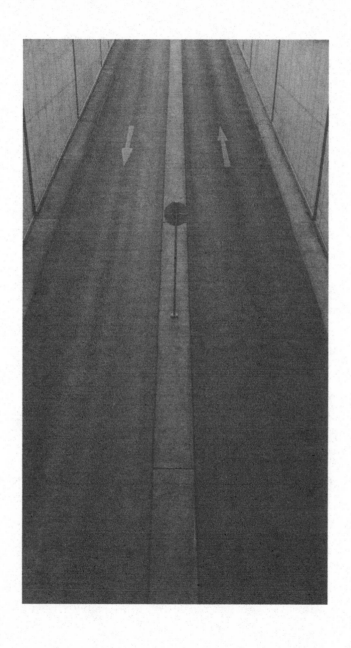

Who Is Driving Your Car?/
Just Let Go

Last night, I dreamt I was the passenger of a car that had no driver. In real life, that scenario would have been terrifying. In my dream, I was calm, breathing cool air from the open window with no fear at all. Although the car was traveling on a busy highway, I felt safe and secure.

Thinking about the dream, the symbolism is very clear to me.

I'd been considering making a serious change in my life for a while, but until recently had not known quite where to start. A series of events had mentally derailed me, and I wanted to take as much time as necessary to understand how to move past the disappointment I felt. After a period of manifestation and hope, an interesting situation presented itself. Even though it was not what I had been considering, I knew instinctively that it was exactly what I needed to do. What could have seemed like a big risk felt like an incredible opportunity. I moved forward without hesitating, and I'm very glad that I did. Sometimes a serendipitous act is essential to move past the blockage. Being open to possibilities could change your entire life. Stepping outside of ordinary activities and choices can be frightening when you aren't sure what's ahead. Trusting your instincts to guide you can seem counterintuitive, but in fact, it is the opposite. In order to grow, one has to take chances.

Looking at the road ahead is uncertain when you don't know what to expect. But knowing and trusting yourself guides your choices, even if you don't know exactly where you're going. You'll be able to make

:nt decisions because instinctively you already know that you are ady to move forward. Humans are very resilient creatures. We have many inner resources that are just waiting to be summoned. When you accept that every part of you is valid and necessary, you open the door to opportunity, love, and growth. You are both the car and the passenger. It is hard to let go of how we think our life should be. So much easier said than done. Surrendering to anything we can't control is uncomfortable. The truth is, the more you try, the less control you have in any situation. It also means that you can't throw your hands up and wait for some kind of divine intervention to make things work out the way you envisioned them. That won't happen either. You have to actually participate by showing up and inviting people and possibilities into your life. Pay attention to your intuition. It is a very good guide.

Many years ago, a friend of mine was happily working in her dream career in the music industry. Suddenly the company closed its doors, leaving her unemployed with a big mortgage. Although my friend had quite a bit of experience, there were few available opportunities in that business at the time. She sent her résumé to every possible employer, but months passed with no success. With a colleague's help, she finally scored an interview at a major record company who offered her a position as an assistant. However, her qualifications were a lot more elevated than entry level status. In addition, the woman she'd be working for had a legendary reputation for mistreating her staff. She felt conflicted. Should she embrace or reject an opportunity?

Deciding not to let pride preclude her possibilities, she accepted the job.

Within three months, her boss was fired. My friend was promoted to the vacated director's position, for which she was perfectly qualified. Years later, she left to build her own company. When she sold it to a global one, they asked her to stay on as a consultant. Her respected skills as a mentor are in high demand and she is living the amazing life she manifested by taking a job that was "beneath her." Resist the ego's desire to meddle with your unlimited potential. Choose to be open to where life leads you. Just let go.

Shifting Your Perspective/
Change Of Scenery

Every experience you have from the time you are born is blueprinted first by family and later reinforced by friends, relatives, teachers, and anyone else you encounter once you go out into the world. It's up to you to revisit those experiences and decide for yourself if you should keep them as they are or view them as lessons to move forward. You can look at all the events in your life positively because no matter what happened in the past, it brought you here today.

As an adult, your future is foreshadowed by your past and present choices. Rather than continuing to travel on the path that you've always taken, you now have the freedom and opportunity to make any detours you like. Why not explore new experiences and open the door to something different than usual? Now is a good time to be adventurous. The people you surround yourself with during these years are a reflection of the way you feel about yourself. By the time you're in your 30's, you'll have a pretty good idea of who you are and where you're headed. You'll have shed a few relationships and gained quite a bit of insight into yourself. You begin to pay attention to what you don't want and are even closer to knowing what you need to feel fulfilled. Moving forward takes perseverance and work, but it's a journey with a lot of rewards. When you shift your perspective toward self-love and acceptance, your healing begins.

We live in a world of instant this, instant that. In fact, pop artist Andy Warhol predicted it in 1968, when he said, "In the future, everyone will be world-famous for 15 minutes." Turns out he was absolutely right. Everyone everywhere can put anything they choose or create on social media, even themselves. Add a side dish of shamelessness to get you even more instafamous. The reality?

15 minutes has had its 15 minutes.

The need to find yourself comes well before you can find others to relate to in a full and present way. It seems clear that if you don't know or accept your true self, you can't expect anyone to know or accept you. Whoever you are today is a compilation of many experiences and choices. You've been navigating your journey with the things you say and do for a long time. Are you satisfied that you are living a healthy, complete life? Maybe you need to stop and reset your compass. It takes courage to look inside yourself and assess that you're better at some things than others. Be honest with your evaluation. Could you work on a few character strengths or change the way you react to situations you can't control? Is there an elephant in the room that needs to be addressed and resolved? I believe that if you stay on the bus long enough, the scenery will change. Whatever is going on in your life is not the end of anything. It's the beginning of discovery. Think about how a conversation you could have with yourself or someone else could move the bus forward.

My Heart Is Open To Love/
Table For One

Love is a word to describe how we feel about someone or something. There are so many uses and meanings that this virtue defies a single definition. It can be positive, like kindness and compassion, or negative, like vanity and egotism. Absolutely anything has the power to stir this emotion in a heartbeat. We love all sorts of things: people, animals, food, art, books, travel. The list is endless. There are a million ways to feel and explore love, but the first and finest is the love you give yourself. Without a foundation, you cannot build a proper home.

The wonderful practice of self-love honors the unique human you are. Embrace the belief that you are worth loving, and your confidence will radiate love into the world where it's most needed. This seemingly tiny action can be incredibly inspirational. When you feel good, your body relaxes and you unconsciously smile. You may not even realize the domino effect of the impact it has on family, friends, and strangers. Unconditional love is the best gift you can give to every part of you. It telegraphs acceptance. Positive affirmation of yourself is an invitation to the world, letting everyone you encounter know that you are open to lead with love in your thoughts and actions.

I know, I know. You've got a cousin, roommate, friend, who would be perfect for me. Thanks, but no thanks. I know I'm not the only one who feels this way. According to a national random sampling of nearly 5000 adults in the US, at least 50% of single people are not interested in a committed romantic relationship or even a date. Why is there a social stigma about this? Is a marriage certificate confirmation of a person's worth? What's up with single-shaming? We don't disparage you for being married!

When I'm in Europe visiting friends, I am often the only single person in a group of couples. It's never been a topic of conversation or speculation, and no one thinks it's weird. During the nine years I lived in the New York suburbs with my son, there were no invitations to parties or dinners. The other mothers at his school had a tight circle that didn't include me. The scarlet letter S marked me as an unwelcome interloper. I was invisible.

I'm not a threat. I don't want your husband. I am quite comfortable on my own in a museum, restaurant, or theatre. I'm not lonely because I'm alone. I happen to enjoy my own company as much as time spent with friends. There is no we in I. Believe it or not, there are plenty of people who just love being single. It's not because we don't think anyone is interested in us, it's because we don't choose to be in a committed romantic relationship. So please, don't fret about me. I am perfectly happy. Are you?

Evolution Revolution/
It All Starts Here

We humans tend to bury the parts of ourselves that we find unpleasant or disagreeable. Instead of looking to hide what we perceive is wrong with us, why not celebrate how each piece of us is actually amazing?

When you accept that no part of you deserves shame, you see that every single bit is what makes you unique and authentic. The traits you think of as flaws are just as important and useful as the traits that you see as extraordinary. A slight shift of your mindset changes a negative experience into a positive one when you embrace the lesson that it teaches you. True love can only be found by having a relationship with yourself that is without conditions or judgements. Opening your heart to accept trust is a transforming acknowledgment of the value of everything that happens on your journey. Believe in the theory that even sudden change brings the gift of growth. As you build a solid foundation for a life that honors you and the people around you, you begin to feel grounded and safe. You are confident in making decisions because you know and like who you are.

Everything you need to live a marvelous existence is within you. A positive relationship with yourself is permission to enjoy a life that moves forward without fear. It invites compassion for you and others, reminding you that joy flows in each of us when we celebrate our individuality. So much of how we respond to others is determined by how we respond to ourselves. If we aren't comfortable with our own selves, we are not healthy enough to give support to anyone else.

We choose our experiences by the energy we put out into the world. Each of us creates a learning pattern that influences our life's path with any decision we make. Every single action has weight and cause. There are no coincidences. Being responsible for the way we live our lives means we must carefully consider the impact of motivation and desire for change.

Disappointment is inevitable if we attempt to control outcomes. Understanding that choice is secondary to reason helps us to review and determine if the option is authentic. It is paramount to consider the actual impetus behind a decision to find resolution or answers. Each of us is born with an inner toolbox full of resources; strengths to help us cope with everyday issues and conflicts.

Once an intention is set, it invokes our essential abilities of intuition, instinct, experience, empathy, and compassion and allows creative energy to flow past the blockages that keep us trapped. Find your power by considering your motivation. Let the challenge be in letting go of preconceived ideas and ideals. Your journey is enhanced by personal choices. It's the difference between surviving and thriving.

Making Lemonade Out Of Lemons/ What Makes You Feel Worthy?

Sometimes people give you a nickname that they think is cute, but no matter how you spin it, a negative nickname is hurtful every time you hear it. Mine was chicken legs because I was very tall and skinny. That wasn't so bad. I've heard a few horror stories from others though. One of my gorgeous friends told me her father called her frog-face. He wanted to spare her from the cruelty of the real world and thought it would teach her that lesson. Instead, she grew up completely convinced that she was hideous. It took years of self-examination and therapy to replace that defeatist judgement with a more accurate one.

Your parents love you, so would they lie? Because their own pattern is skewed. I believe you either embrace or reject the patterns you grow up learning. If you want to replace the inaccurate assessment that you got at home or school with a positive and fitting affirmation of yourself, it's absolutely necessary to accept your own power to repattern the blueprint. Look at the words people have said to you and about you. How do they make you feel? Think about why people would say them to you. Decide for yourself if it is actually a true evaluation. How do they make you feel when you hear them now? Can you replace that word with a more honest and positive one?

My friend told me that she realized it was her father's way of trying to protect her. She now looks at it differently and with compassion for his limitations, able to let go of the hurtful nickname that isn't the slightest bit true. Shifting her perception of a simple word changed the power of it. By releasing the emotional charge that it caused in the past, she was able to see her authentic self clearly. Our lives are so complicated! The choices we make to feel comfortable within ourselves and good about who we are often get tangled up between mind and body. What do you see when you look in the mirror when you're by yourself, with nothing and no one to guide you? Do you respect that person?

Achieving an appreciation of your own worth requires a very introspective visit to your inner toolbox. Feeling grounded and comfortable with who you are is peaceful because the experience of gratefulness for your actions is realistic and honest. Mistakes become valuable lessons when you shift your perspective to replace blame with compassion. Every action brings a consequence, and careful consideration can alter an outcome positively or negatively.

Mandela said hatred is like drinking poison and waiting for it to kill your enemy. True, that. Redemption is achieved when you forgive yourself and others. Everyone deserves a do-over if they are truly sorry. I would not like to be judged by who I was even five years ago, would you? If you hold yourself responsible and make appropriate reparations, it allows you to let go of limitations that hold you back from appreciating yourself and others.

Choosing to be ethical requires an acceptance of humanity and decency. Do the right thing in every situation. Use your behavior to reflect your values and ethics, no matter whether you believe in a Supreme Being or not. The shared bond of a like-minded community furthers personal well-being and the quality of life for everyone. You are one of kind, yet one of many. Humans are a tribe. Kindness and care also go a long way on the journey to an authentic self. Tolerance and generosity are powerful tools. A positive attitude is essential to enjoy life. Each of us needs to give and feel love to be whole. Following these simple guidelines helps us to embrace each other and move together solidly on a strong foundation of genuine love.

You Can Avoid Everything Except Taxes, Death . . . And Change/ Numbness Is Not An Option

There's no way to avoid it. The more you try, the less success you'll have. Change will find you, no matter how well you hide. You'll have to find a way to accommodate it. How you respond to unexpected or proposed events can alter your whole life. It's easier to make changes when you are not in a position to be challenged. Your choices can actually help you to reevaluate the way you live. To create a positive outcome, take the time to figure out what is truly important to you.

Life is both long and short. If you're happy with yourself, it flies by. There's never enough time. If you're unhappy with your choices, life is an endless stream of disappointments and chaos. What do you want to achieve? Do you have goals and dreams? When you have direction and focus, you open yourself to your authentic purpose. The best thing about change is that it is not fixed. You can move on from anything if you're flexible and patient.

Let go of the negative cycle of regret for any missed opportunities or decisions you've made in the past. Those are the lessons that taught you how to be prepared for the new ones that will be coming your way. Learning from the past is the gift those chances gave you to be able to make better choices in the present and for your future. Be good to your mind and body. Choose to live a balanced life with the food you consume and a daily physical exercise routine. Taking care of yourself promotes positivity and health, making you feel better about yourself and the world around you. Take a walk through your neighborhood or a hike in the hills. Do Pilates or yoga. Meditate. Enjoy the weather and the fresh air. Breathe!

Live a full life by facing some of the things that cause you to feel anxious. I'm not suggesting that you jump out of a plane (unless, of course, that's on your list of things to master), but certainly, there are smaller fears you can conquer. For me, standing at a podium to speak in front of a group was anxiety-producing until the day my smart, solution-oriented friend Raquelle suggested that I sit in a chair with the audience. I don't know why I didn't think of that myself. The moment she said it, I knew she was right. Her few words changed my life. I sit in the circle now and it feels great. Take back your power!

Don't worry about what other people think. The fear of judgement from others is a waste of time. Apologize if you hurt someone's feelings, but don't apologize for any benign legal behavior that makes you feel good about yourself. Dance spontaneously in public when you hear your jam on a store's sound system. Sing karaoke, especially if you're tone-deaf. My Vegas friend told me whenever anyone sings *Piano Man* by Billy Joel, the whole crowd joins in, so even if you sing badly it'll be fun. I'm pretty sure it's a requirement of self-love and acceptance to enjoy yourself. Go for it!

You're the change you need to make. Love yourself and explore the possibilities! When you are in crisis, it may seem easier to run instead of dealing with what makes you feel sad. Using alcohol or drugs to self-medicate is only a temporary relief. Avoiding the cause of your suffering neglects the total experience of being human. It may seem counterintuitive, but grief or sadness can actually be good for you. It is appropriate to feel every emotion in order to heal and grow with new wisdom. Your ability to love yourself is essential to understanding the importance of every strength and difference in your inner toolbox.

When you are able to accept yourself, it becomes easier to invite others into your tribe. Surrender to the process by recognizing that whatever sadness you feel can be aided by confronting it. Part of the discovery of the authentic self is this emotional journey. Think of a past situation when you felt adrift in a psychological crisis. As you look back on it, can you see how it was actually a step forward? Every experience, no matter how difficult, brings something good into your life, even if you don't see it at the time. Everyone feels pain. Facing your suffering and processing it is a very powerful transformation.

The Commission Of Humanity/ Leaning In

Humanity is a virtue symbolizing human love and compassion toward others. The scholarly philosophy of basic human dignity was created in the 13th century to explain the necessity of human rights. Certain standards of behavior are meant to be inalienable. A person is inherently entitled to them simply because he or she is a human being regardless of age, ethnic, origin, location, language, religion, or any other status.

So, what has happened to us?

Have we stopped caring about the things that make us connect to each other? Have we lost the very essence of selflessness that connects us? Or did we never truly embrace it? Let's be honest. There will always be people who have more and those who have less. The world is neither equal nor fair. Does that make us better, lesser, or simply different? Don't we want to care for others and have others who care about us? Of course, we do. Our empathy is necessary for the survival of the human race.

We have a great capacity to love others. We don't need to judge. The welfare of each of us is important and has value. Let's shift humanity toward an understanding and respect for each other. We can do this. It will help us to focus on the needs of others, rather than our own. Let's stop ignoring our humanity. Make a decision and commitment to open your mind and heart. Indivisible. We are one.

Are you so self-sufficient that expressing the need to lean on someone right now seems ridiculous? You may not actually realize how deeply you are craving affection. Happiness depends on one's ability to love and express the need for love. There are so many people you love and who love you. Have you told your partner, your children, or friends how much you love them lately?

Connection is everything for humans. It makes you feel good to hug and be hugged. Even virtually. We often get caught up in our own heads and forget about how much we need to reach out to the other people in our lives. This particular time is divisive for everyone. You can express your feelings in a conversation or a letter. It's important to let others know how much they mean to you. You'll see how much you mean to them.

Out Of Control/Changing From The Inside Out

Who is in charge of your life? Understanding your limitations will help you to make choices that you might not otherwise consider. When you feel the most out of control, you are actually the most in control. What is essential is that you trust the way things are happening without trying to manipulate the outcome.

Use your intuition to release fears and judgements. Surrender to the awareness that choices you make may not always appear logical or practical at the time. Call on your faith and confidence to be open to accepting guidance as you prepare to move forward. No one has the divine power to decide exactly how or when things will happen, but if you believe in your ability to manifest your goals, the only limitations are ones you place on yourself. When you don't judge yourself, the power of others to judge you dissipates.

Consider the option of stillness. Sitting with yourself is a good way to let your mind and body connect. Everything that happens is part of your journey. If you look back on your life so far, you can see how certain events were changed when you tried to manage them in a way that conflicted with your true self. As you continue on your path to wholeness, you begin to realize that human life is a jigsaw puzzle. Each piece that you connect to another eventually forms a beautiful and complete picture.

You change your outside self with the clothes you choose, but have you put the same thought and energy into changing your inside self? Look carefully at the patterns of behavior that you have chosen so far. Are you truly happy with who you are? Are any of the choices ones you have unconsciously mirrored or accepted without considering your own options? Find the answer to this question by asking yourself what you want and where you're going.

Set yourself free of an old blueprint that doesn't serve who you are or aspire to be. Begin the transformation right now, at this very moment. Today. Use your inner toolbox to open your mind and surrender to an acceptance of your entire being. Acknowledging all of your traits is not giving up who you are. It's the most honest way to examine every part of you without judgement. Instead of regretting past actions, find gratitude for each of your characteristics because you need them. They are all useful to you. Understand that your whole self is part of a bigger connection that requires willingness to see the truth without excuses.

Give yourself the opportunity to revive and regenerate respect for yourself. Lean on intuition to achieve liberation from old actions. Your true value is in your appreciation of yourself. You are the only you, a unique and valuable part of the world. You are not your clothes or your car or your home. Knowing your inner self is the only way to affect positive change. Humility is an important part of overcoming any obstacles in your path. Loving yourself begins the journey toward freedom and finding your purpose. Shift your perception and expectations to reflect the compassion you deserve.

Is The Life You're Living Really Working For You?/ When Pigs Fly

Honestly, I don't know why anyone does anything. We all self-sabotage and lose hope, not realizing that nothing happens without desire, even if it's subconscious. Everything occurs for a reason, although sometimes the motive may seem elusive. The best way to maintain hope is to let go of ego and repattern your old blueprint. Be ready to embrace the truth of who you are.

Are you happy with the choices you have made? Do you regret decisions you made in the past? Those actions brought you to an acceptance and understanding of the person you have grown into. They formed the foundation you stand on and gave you the power that can lead you to become a whole and authentic person. Why carry the heavy stones of old judgements when you can leave them behind? Every mistake you make has a positive aspect as a valuable teaching tool. If you feel you have failed in some way, reboot your ability to see those missteps as a reason to rethink your behavior and let it propel you forward. Start by deconstructing the life you have led up to this moment. Pain is often necessary on the journey to fulfillment and peace, but experience is a wise teacher. Everything is possible when you surrender to honesty. Releasing the darkness you carry lets the light in. Open the door to love. Watch it flood in and carry you forward. When you love yourself, you make it feasible for others to love you and be loved by you.

Optimism is the ability to believe and envision that when something negative happens, it's because something even better is about to come along. It's the thing that holds hope in our hearts, making it both valuable and powerful. Instead of fearing the worst, it's an expectation that a superior outcome is probable. It's a whole lot better than pessimism, which is very draining and hard to be around (i.e., Pooh's friend Eeyore). Even realism can get a bad rap because the truth, no matter how logical it seems, has a way of deflating dreams and suggesting that it's better to be safe than sorry. There will always be an argument against anything that sounds a bit off the beaten path. Fear has a pervasive grip on possibility. Delusional optimism holds the certainty that things will improve and never go from bad to worse. It expects without doubt that, despite all evidence to the contrary, predictability is moot. It's a definite. You will experience the greatest, most fantastic, marvelous thing, and there's absolutely no reason to think otherwise. It simply cannot fail.

I sort of see the sense in a bit of delusional optimism. Why not? If you have an idea that you firmly believe in but others think is crazy or unattainable, there are small steps you can take to move the dream forward. It might take a while, but if you are clear about your vision, learn from your mistakes, and adapt your actions to further the goal, it's possibly achievable. Study your business plan. Decide how to make the first move, then go to the next, and so on. Make sure you stay on target with your belief. Even if it feels a bit shameless, use every contact you have. The key to success is action. If you believe it's true and are willing to put the work in, it will surely happen. After all, you're the delusional optimist!

Universal Connection Starts With You/I'm Fine aka A Silent Cry For Help

It's easy to feel disconnected from others when emotional or physical neglect was your experience as a child. When you don't know why human connection is necessary to become whole, you shut down from getting the support you need to form healthy relationships as an adult.

How do you break the negative cycle? Compassion. Patience. Understanding. Love.

You let go of old patterns and judgements, get to know your true self, and create a more accurate blueprint of who you are. Finding joy in the discovery of your authentic self is the path to self-love and acceptance. Even when it's hard to be honest, acknowledge that every part of you is valuable and deserves respect. An essential connection to yourself teaches you that being alone isn't the slightest bit lonely.

When you take responsibility for yourself and your choices, you are able to choose what you want to change as well as what you accept in yourself and others. Your purpose becomes clear because you have broken the negative cycle of blame and despair. Shifting your perspective opens many possibilities, even some you don't know about yet. You heal.

This transformation gives you the power to experience your worth. It frees you to embrace inner confidence and happiness. A positive attitude draws people to your tribe. Your good energy frees you from the fear of rejection and negativity. Forming relationships will be easier because you know who you are. When someone asks you how you are, do you automatically say, "I'm fine?" Take a moment to look at yourself and be honest. Are you *actually* fine or do you just want to stuff the annoying voice in your head that judges you? Your true self makes no judgements. However, your ego (aka monkey mind) loves judging you. It preys on any tiny insecurity within you that it can uncover. It is constantly talking to you, telling you to watch out for that guy, don't trip on the curb, you shouldn't eat that . . . etc.

In order to bypass your chattering monkey mind, you have to examine and accept each of your personality's quirks and characteristics. This is the path to your authentic self. The more you get to know yourself, the simpler it is to accept and love every part of you. Once you have embraced your own humanness, it becomes easier to understand and accept other people. It helps you to stop judging them for the things you don't like in yourself. Forgiveness is possible with insight. It's also not shameful to admit that you can't do everything by yourself. It takes a lot of help to make it on your own. I believe that you have a whole tribe of people who would love to be there for you, if you ask.

I'm always happy to be asked to help. I will definitely do what I can. A lot of people have helped, and do help me. I'm grateful for their assistance. It's the way our world should work, but we may need to be reminded to be here for each other.

And no one can read your mind.

So, speak up!

We all have issues.

We all need kindness.

We all need balance.

We all have the tools in our inner toolbox to move forward and achieve a full and wonderful life.

Find your inner ability to empathize with someone. Understanding and sharing go a long way. By using love and compassion as a guide, you greet the world from a courageous and empowered place that inspires others to do the same. Your anxieties will recede if you have the confidence to know and claim all of yourself. It's freeing to be open and accepting. No one can tell you who you are when you know who you are. Ask for help if you need it. It's a powerful and positive energy that works both ways.

May I Have Your Attention, Please?
(Finding Problems In Solutions)/
The Egotistic Mind
(Twinkle, Little Star)

Let's look at the shadow side of attention seeking. Perhaps you're trapped in a work environment where you feel ostracized or marginalized, or in a relationship that isn't nurturing or supportive. It's an overwhelming feeling of impending doom that you don't know how to fix or escape.

So, you turn to the Internet to find others who share a similar discomfort—a friend or two with whom you can be open and not judged. There must be lots of people in the world who'd like to be noticed for their unique qualities and not ridiculed for their differences. A tribe of invisible humans like you.

And with this hope, you've joined social media sites, unprepared for the vicious attacks of the ubiquitous online trolls; the bullies of every sort adept at bringing complete strangers down a peg or two for the unabashed joy of watching their dopamine drop. You'll never know when, how, or why, but you will feel the sting of many random blows.

Do you wonder how they can judge someone they've never met, call them names, and label them? Because hurting you is their dopamine. Their momentary high. Their rush. And unless your ego is uber strong, it's another hurt you'll add to your ever-growing mountain of pain.

Bottom line.

Social media breeds contempt for achievement. If you're going to participate, you have to embrace who you are, shadow side and all. If they smell vulnerability, the buzzards pounce. Laugh at yourself. Be humble. Be you. We are human. It's a mad world. Find pleasure in both your foibles and your successes. Don't worry about what others think because you know who you are.

Start now.

A strong ego is the bright flashlight necessary to navigate human darkness. Why do we need attention from strangers? Because it's fun to be the center of the universe, even briefly. We like it, no matter how loudly we protest. Say something clever and everyone laughs. It feels good, right? Until it doesn't.

When the lights suddenly go dark, and you are alone with yourself, remember that you are not defined by other people's assessments. You alone choose your goals and your path. If you know who you are, any slings and arrows will bounce off. Your inner self is waiting to be free. Move forward and feel the power of your own strength.

Understanding Yourself/
Everything Has Value

Sometimes we look harshly at others when the behavior they are modeling is actually behavior we don't like about ourselves. It's hard to look inward sometimes, so we often don't. It may seem counterintuitive to embrace what we consider negative qualities about ourselves. It's not a bad thing to accept, own, and move forward from patterns. I remember being ignored at school. I was quiet, introverted, and never joined in groups.

As a child, my professor father told me to go to my room after school, do my homework, and read a book. In our home, sports of any kind were looked down upon as a waste of time. As a result, I never participated in any activities during my school years. I accepted his judgement that people played sports because they lacked the intelligence to contribute anything worthwhile to the world.

As an adult, it's a giant realization to discover that everything I have ever done has been a solo endeavor. I've never worked with others. I've always dismissed opportunities to join a team. Why? I'm not sure. Maybe I didn't think my opinions would matter to others, or arrogantly dismissed game participants as stupid. Is it possible that I accepted the blueprint I was given because I was afraid of how others would view me?

I've spent most of my work life without close interaction, and when I have worked with others, I still did my job alone, usually in a factory with people who spoke very little English. Flash forward.

Now I am part of a collective of amazing women who have had very different lives and experiences than me. They are fascinating, interesting, and challenging. My life has been enriched beautifully by the very things I chose to ignore. I'm doing things I would never have thought of trying, and I'm having fun. I feel part of a valuable team and my life is so much better for it. It's ok to forgive yourself for choices and behavior that you have dragged around for a long time. Maybe, in the past, you needed protection or comfort. Once you've accepted how it negatively affects your happiness, why not let it go?

It is a good idea to look at behaviors in others that are upsetting to you. It could just be that the thing that bothers you about them is also something you don't like about yourself. Look back at the negative events throughout your life and begin to see them as lessons. Understand that those experiences allow you to make more satisfying choices now because of the way they affected you. Rather than letting them paralyze or prohibit you from moving forward, release them with love, knowing that they brought you to this place. You can be grateful to your past for giving you this gift. Taking responsibility and letting darkness go brings clarity and invites positivity.

Every part of your journey brings you to where you need to be. Along the way, you encounter setbacks and possibilities. Making peace with your past affects your future. Let the love begin in your heart. Start with yourself.

When It Rains, Look For Rainbows/ How Do You Set Boundaries?

If you ask me what my greatest fear is, I'll answer with conviction: disappointment. I never want to let anyone down, and I have a lot of difficulty understanding how people can do it to me. Of course, things happen that are beyond anyone's control, but when you have the ability to shift the way you view the sadness it causes, it becomes easier to manage the pain.

How you come to terms with disappointment speaks to your character. If your expectations are too high, the possibility of being triggered is heightened. Lowering your expectations will definitely help you to accept that reality doesn't always have a happy ending. It takes strength to look at what happened and to make a rational and calm decision to move forward without losing hope.

Sometimes you don't even realize what actually made you feel the loss because you are still subconsciously hanging on to what you wanted or expected. When hopes and dreams are dashed by unrealistic expectations, feeling depressed and immobilized by anger or frustration is imminent. Reflecting allows a calmer experience and the resolve to disconnect in a healthy way. If you didn't get what you wished for, use inner delusional optimism to assume it's because something better is coming your way. This is an opportunity to re-examine your goals. Consider this setback a learning tool to achieve the success you desire. Progress is possible.

Reality squelches disappointment when you choose to see a situation through the positive lens of what can be, not what should have been.

It is important to create boundaries. It can be hard to let other people know that their behavior is not okay, without feeling defensive. Setting strong boundaries may feel rigid because you don't want to disappoint others, but disappointing yourself emotionally shuts you down and clouds your clarity.

Putting yourself first is not only healthy, it's necessary for self-esteem and growth. If you are being mistreated or shamed, protecting your well-being and integrity is paramount. If someone tries to make you choose between yourself and them, it's not a choice.

Weigh your own needs before considering the needs of others. Take the time to look carefully at all options before making a decision. Define your personal boundaries in relationships by claiming the right to care for yourself first, then select the action that most comfortably works for you. If you feel confident in the way you address your own care, it becomes easy to think about how you'll respond to a friend or family member when they ask for your help. Count on your inner strength and compassion to help you decide how you will answer them.

Setting limits doesn't obligate you to reply in a certain way because you are afraid of the consequences. It challenges you to pause and consider your response with kindness and regard for your own limits. An open heart and compassion do not mean compliance. Understanding and connection thrive when you connect with yourself. It feels good to step up authentically and honestly to own your choices. A healthy boundary is one that is chosen with sensitivity toward yourself and others.

How Do You Stop Judging Yourself?/Climbing Out Of The Rabbit Hole

You learn to love every part of yourself because when you accept all of yourself, there is no good or bad. You are able to compassionately see others as individuals trying to navigate life, just as you are. You accept that if you don't love yourself, you can't love others. Once you activate your natural free will, you'll begin to move forward comfortably within yourself and that essence is what you will send into the world. It's just a matter of shifting your *need* for acceptance to actual acceptance. You can alter any outcome if you shift your perspective.

Try looking at things a bit differently. The way you respond to challenging situations can transform your entire life. When you adjust a pattern that you have followed in the past, you open yourself to the understanding that what you've always believed may no longer serve your needs now. Letting go of stagnant behaviors is a step toward positive change and acceptance.

Depression and hopelessness in our society is a universal experience. Sometimes the emotional stresses of just being human can feel negative and heavy. Everyone suffers from episodes of debilitating damage at different points in life. It is unavoidable. The way you accept and grieve loss or betrayal is an indication of how necessary the path to transformative healing is for your growth. The process can only happen when you embrace self-discovery by choosing not to avoid or numb your pain. Facing a crisis requires being open to confronting it.

In many cases, people are greatly helped with some sort of treatment. Emotional issues may require medication or therapy with a counselor or professional. Others are soothed with meditation and self-reflection. Talking with trusted friends or loved ones can also assist in your ability to recognize what you need.

The surrender to acceptance and forgiveness of the original source of pain begins a steady climb out of the rabbit hole. Allow yourself to examine your challenge authentically and truthfully. Let it go with love and compassion. The capability and capacity to move forward is through forgiveness and a full understanding that your wholeness is essential. Reset your pattern. You deserve to heal.

Why are you trying so hard to fit in when you were born to stand out?

—Ian Wallace

An Outlier's Dream/If I Only Had The Nerve . . .

How important is your belief system to the universe? Your lifestyle speaks to who you are and what you hold to be essential. Sharing your message takes careful thought and planning to make a serious impact. Allowing others to recognize themselves through the words and deeds you champion opens the door to like-minded people who accept your values but also to criticism and shame if you are careless or glib.

Since you are literally your own brand, the way you market yourself tells the world how unique you are. To consider who and what you want to align yourself with and to successfully gain influence and trust requires the courage to speak authentically. Define and share what you are passionate about. Are your choices inspirational or aspirational? Allow others to see themselves in your paradigm. Don't restrict yourself to old models that are outdated. Discover interesting ways to build your interests into self-actualization of your personal principles and achievements.

The Internet is an opportunity for anyone and everyone who has something to say. Your words have weight that guarantee both positive and negative reactions. Think carefully about attaching yourself to any discipline that doesn't speak to your own creed of ethics. Create buzz by crafting your particular philosophy. Your mind holds the key to the door of possibilities. Be bold. Be brave. Be original.

Sometimes, holding on to your authentic self is tested by the masses. Moral courage happens when you choose to do what you believe is right, no matter what the consequences may be. There are many ways this virtue can be fostered and maintained if you are strong enough to hold on to your views. The natural tendency toward fear is overcome when conviction is displayed.

Standing alone can be a risk in our society. It may feel shameful or cause the loss of friends, even a job. Worrying about what other people think is common. No one wants to be called out and humiliated. At the same time, it speaks to one's character when a personal opinion or belief takes precedence over a more popular group choice or decision. Considering the consequences of maintaining integrity while coping with outside challenges is highly individual and requires honesty to determine that this choice is a courageous effort to do the right thing in the face of adversity. In the end, the fight between fear and courage is one that is present in daily life. Deciding if standing up for what you believe is more important than being popular is for you to determine. Who you are is built on a foundation of these circumstances and choices.

Serenity Now!/Patience Is A Virtue

The way you choose to experience stress affects everything in your life. It's not easy to change the relationship you have with yourself, but the practice of meditation can certainly help. When you are able to sit still and clear your mind of distracting thoughts that pull you out of being present, the ability to observe a situation in a nonjudgmental way allows clarity to help with understanding. Making a major shift in your approach to life requires a certain kind of mindfulness to embrace calm.

Focusing on your breathing and body instead of your wishes and wants allows true feelings to come in and out without automatic habits or responses. You can shift the way you react by releasing yourself from an old pattern of behavior. A difficult situation will be monitored by observing carefully before acting negatively.

This sort of technique takes time and diligence to embrace, but the physical health benefits are worth the effort. Anger, anxiety, eating disorders, and suicidal tendencies can be better managed if controlling thoughts are addressed and diffused before you react. It may take professional help to achieve, but beginning a daily practice of mind-body awareness is integral to wellness. Self-care is a choice. The possibilities can change your entire life and connection to authentic self and personal happiness.

Watching a circumstance unfold helps you to know when to act. It's a way of being in touch with your inner toolbox of intuition. It's quite freeing to develop a calm practice of waiting, where you can trust yourself to let go of the need to control a frustrating situation. It's not procrastination when the ultimate satisfaction is in reaching your desired goal without unnecessary conflict.

If you step back to assess possibilities and outcomes, you're able to carefully approach an issue and spend the necessary time to look at it without giving up or giving in. Being able to sit with yourself and not demand immediate results gives you power.

However, waiting is hard, especially since modern life constantly reminds us that anything we want is instantly and immediately available at all times. A considered choice to accept gratitude for what we have helps the management of expectations. Being mindful makes your journey worthwhile and wonderful.

Take a minute to decide if what you want is actually what you need. Count to ten before asking yourself to stop and honestly consider the consequences of your actions. Speak after you have heard the thought in your own head. Before it leaves your lips, do you really want to say it? Or do it? Is your reaction worth it? Slow down and let things happen as they should in their own time. Be your own advocate and handle your day-to-day stresses with compassion and humor. Nothing is that important. You've got this. Now breathe!

We Need To Listen To What's Not Being Said/Silence Is Golden

When a family member, friend, or co-worker is silently suffering a stressful time, are we 100% available to reassure them that they are not alone? Or are we too busy managing or avoiding our own problems during this unexpected quarantine? There are so many current pressures that cause tension and strain for us. Especially with this new world order hanging over us like the sword of Damocles, we need to quickly learn how to navigate getting along with family members and working from home. Even the most loving of tribes gets fed up with each other in close quarters 24/7.

Additionally, money worries and food shortages consume us daily. How to get employment, pay bills? Forget about saving money. We have bigger fears of late, like running out of toilet paper and sanitizer! We have to constantly remember that we actually need each other to survive. Situations can be diffused or resolved by discussing them with friends, family, partners, or even the people involved. We have Face-Time, Skype, Zoom. Even the telephone.

The more serious conversations require introspection and maybe even online counseling to move forward. There is no such thing as closure if someone you love is gravely injured or dies. Whenever your world changes in an unexpected way, sadness is rampant and often, hopelessness ensues. Let's remember that we are all in this together. We can use this time to develop more empathy and kindness for the people around us. Even the people we don't know who need our help, like the food bank or your elderly neighbor who would appreciate you remembering she could use a carton of milk. Let's think outside of ourselves and pay it forward.

Do you say what you mean and mean what you say? Most of our communications are nonverbal, so what you're saying is not nearly as important as what you're not saying. What are the messages your body language is sending out? If you notice that you smile or laugh when you are actually feeling sad, the message you are communicating to the outside world is inauthentic to your true self. How do you truly feel about what you are experiencing? Are you hiding "negative" traits because you think others won't like you if they see the real you? No matter how you react in a situation, all your feelings are useful. They help you to understand and accept yourself fully.

If you are comfortable with yourself, it makes it possible for the rest of the world to be comfortable with you. Staying faithful to who you are without judgement accelerates growth and tolerance in yourself and others. When the only approval you need is your own, you give yourself the power and permission to move forward.

There is no part of you that is bad. Value your strengths and accept what you previously considered weaknesses as qualities that are helpful and necessary. Turn them into positive affirmations of your personality. What makes you unique is how you interpret the events in your life. Be honest and open with yourself and let the healing begin.

If You Want To Change The World, Start With You/Do Unto Others

In the midst of enforced social distancing, it has become ironically clear that what we need most is connection. The further we move away from each other, the less empathy we feel for anything outside ourselves. We become too hyper-focused on our own needs and discomfort to consider others. Our perspective is preoccupied with what has been taken away and what we have lost. The freedom and choice to live our lives the way we choose has shifted.

Yet, a closer examination reveals what we have gained. We have both opportunity and obligation to reset the world. We can use this time to give every human the same choices that many of us take for granted. These seemingly simple things are a constant consideration to people who are different from us, and it's neither right nor fair.

Real change requires reflection and recalibration of core choices and values. Just by opening our hearts, we are embracing the chance to educate ourselves and create a new world where there is only one human race. If we lay down the old paradigms and move forward with empathy and kindness and treat others as we would like to be treated, we can do it.

If we each look inside ourselves to accept this powerful challenge, we will see change. How your behavior affects others is something we've been forced to think about more than ever since COVID-19. There are people who feel the virus is a political posture that doesn't exist or adamantly refuse to wear a mask or practice social distance. They believe that their inalienable human rights and civil liberties are being taken away.

This outrage and defiance are made even more controversial because of the daily conflicting reports and opinions. All the guidelines and mandates in the world won't matter unless we accept that this virus isn't going to go away quickly—and maybe not at all—unless we start to consider the lives of other people as important as our own.

Quarantine affects everyone. As unpleasant as it is to be separated from others, the secondary consequences of ignoring the obvious dangers are far worse. When the Spanish flu was ravaging America in 1918, needless deaths occurred due to the formation of the Anti-Mask League of San Francisco. Many people refused to wear masks, impacting the health of innocent people. The ensuing trauma was heartbreaking but preventable. Is this who we really are?

How would you feel if it were you who had a compromised health condition and someone's decision affected you? What about your grandparents, mothers, fathers, sisters, brothers, children, friends, co-workers? Is it more real when it's personal? We share the ability to choose compassion and behavior that benefits everyone. Cultivating our connection to others by showing kindness and care is something every single one of us can practice daily. It's called humanity.

Give-And-Take/Drawing A Line In The Sand

There seem to be people who want to help everyone but have difficulty letting anyone help them, even if they really need it. We don't understand why they won't accept our help. Could it be that they are unwilling to resolve their situation or problem or that they don't feel they deserve it? Some people even ignore what they need in order to help others because it's more comfortable for them to give than to receive. It's a frustrating common scenario. Humans!

Being independent does not mean that you don't need or accept help or that you owe someone a debt because they've done something for you. It feels good to occasionally do something nice for a family member, friend, or stranger for absolutely no reason. It also feels delightful to receive a serendipitous gift from someone unexpectedly. Another person may be able to help you because your need is easy for them in a way that is difficult for you. Your problem that seems insurmountable might be no big deal to them. They may even feel honored if you ask for their support.

Years ago, I was having a hard time financially but felt embarrassed asking for assistance. A good friend who owned a neighborhood restaurant saw that I was struggling, even though I had never told him. Many nights he'd ask me to join him for dinner so he wouldn't have to eat alone. We both knew the truth. To this day, I have never forgotten his kindness. When he needed a favor years later, I was able to be there for him. I felt as good then as when he had helped me. Somehow things always work out if you're open to letting them.

If you need or can give aid, why not?

One small kindness that could change everything for someone may mean very little for you to give. In the same way, if you need a small kindness, I bet there is someone in your life who would love to give to you—if you let them know. Respecting each other enough to offer or accept the help you need without shame or guilt is what true friendship is about.

Setting clear boundaries creates healthy relationships. It's important to know who you are and where you stand in order to protect yourself from anyone telling you who you should be. Separating your feelings from another person's helps you to make decisions based on your authentic needs. It ensures a lifetime of honest and fulfilling relationships. important to know who you are and where you stand in order to protect yourself from anyone telling you who you should be. Separating your feelings from another person's helps you to make decisions based on your authentic needs. It ensures a lifetime of honest and fulfilling relationships.

Conversely, when you take responsibility for someone else, you are not allowing them the right to experience their own emotions. Insinuating your judgements to manipulate or influence their choices is as harmful as deflecting your own needs to please someone. Either is a violation of one's personal code, causing resentment toward either party. The decision to use your instincts to identify red flags and empower your choice of actions is crucial to your well-being.

Self-esteem and individuality are defined by the value you place on yourself. Consider what could make you want to please another person at the expense of sacrificing your identity. Fearing judgement or hurting someone's feelings is not a good reason to bury your true feelings. You are entitled and encouraged to decide what behaviors you will or will not accept from the people you let into your life. Listen to your gut, your inner voice. Your happiness is solely your responsibility. Only you possess the ability to act when your boundaries are being crossed.

How Do You Feel?/Balance

It's a good daily practice to check in with yourself and ask this simple question. Passively awaiting change is unfulfilling and disappointing. Unless you actively sit with your feelings and listen to your gut (i.e., your inner voice), you'll miss the opportunity to discover if you're reacting or genuinely reflecting. Resetting expectations and experiences is a positive life-changing decision. First, release your mind from engaging in thoughts or actions. Take a few deep breaths to clear it of trying to control outcomes. Allow your heart and body to experience whatever comes into your mind without preconceived notions or judgements.

Free will gives you the advantage of choice in any situation. It's your hidden superpower. You don't need to repeat a difficult memory if you replace it with a better one. Negative experiences have a way of reminding us to be fearful, to protect ourselves by attaching limitations that don't serve us. Resolution takes full mind-body engagement to undo an automatic response without forgetting the valuable lesson you learned. Use your toolbox to help let go of previous experiences that are attached to your present blueprint. Once you understand that you are in total control of your feelings, you can choose to connect to a pleasant outcome instead.

Repattern your thinking. Allow your heart to make choices along with your mind. Rational solutions need compassion and empathy in the same way that emotions need to be acknowledged. Each needs the other for true guidance. So . . . how do you feel? An emotional decision can feel powerful but not necessarily an accurate reflection of your true self. The same is true of a decision made solely with mental energy, which may be a response motivated by fear to avoid or deflect pain. How your head manages what your heart feels needs to be a balance of mind and spirit to be effective and positive. Making choices that promote change breaks repetitive patterns.

Be prepared and open for what will come next. You can guide your internal energies by paying attention to both what you want and what you need. Uniting hope with action reflects courage to accept healthier choices. Moving forward requires you to trust that letting go of your desire to control outcomes will strengthen and not weaken you. It is an organic way to develop your real self.

Trust your intuition to lead you. It is often easier to remain in the comfortable discomfort of where you are than to leave the safety of the familiar for the wilds of the unknown. Breaking the cycle is the only way to let go of an old blueprint, but the reward is an authentic life. When your natural energies work together, it's an enlightening experience to see how well they get along and observe what they can accomplish. Fear precludes possibilities and shuts them out. Courage invites them in. Manifest your life's purpose with clarity and conviction.

The Mind Is A Terrible Thing To Waste/How Do I Heal?

Full disclosure: I talk to myself. It's no big deal, just a silent loop of possibilities and realities. Please don't call my therapist. I'm not alone. Studies show that it's common to carry on a running conversation with yourself either in your head or verbally. My friend Diane says she prefers to talk to her dogs, who are always happy and don't judge. I think that's a great alternative, too. Either way, you're still listening to your thoughts.

Many people have an inner dialogue, but apparently not everyone. I personally find it helpful to run sentences in my head as a way of editing decisions. Sometimes there's a bit of an argument or debate going on up in there, but it always gets sorted out before it turns into a melee. Listening to yourself can be useful if you count on your own voice to guide you in decisions and beliefs.

What would life be like without our box of tools to keep us moving forward? Besides the mundane day-to-day minutiae of whether to eat cold cereal or oatmeal, my inner narrative reminds me to consider topic options for my growing tome, or reach out to a friend I'm thinking about. I rely on my subconscious mind to organically organize the way I process information, so the chirping of the chattering voices is welcome. I can't imagine what I would do if my little chorus suddenly went quiet. Thankfully, they're full of opinions about everything.

There was a lot of chaos around me as a child, so I spent a lot of time in my room reading and listening to music. Whenever the noise got too loud, or the words too hurtful, my mind escaped to a refuge where I felt safe, a place that belonged to me alone. My shelter flourished as I added details from books I'd read or places I wanted to visit. It grew into a huge forest with a clearing in the middle. I could sit on soft earth as bright colored birds sang, watching sunlight dance on the flowing stream that separated my forest from the rest of the world.

As the years went by, my sanctuary became even more detailed and private. I no longer noticed the darkness on the other side of the stream. I strung long ropes of twinkling fairy lights through the trees. At the top of the tallest tree where the full moon rested, I could see the Big Dipper and Orion's Belt in my purple velvet sky of bright stars.

I often visit my forest.

I can be there anytime I need or want. I just close my eyes and open my mind. It's a calming oasis in moments of stress or anxiety.

This is how I heal. How do you heal?

The Cure For Boredom Is Curiosity/Curiosity Killed The Cat

I've been hearing a lot from friends about their ensuing boredom during COVID-19. The current restrictions have rendered us immobile and frustrated. It is true that we are unable to participate in many of the activities we used to take for granted. However, there is a simple solution to the ennui we're feeling. We can do anything we dream of if we just pay attention to our intuition.

What is it you want to accomplish? Decide to engage in your life and take charge. Begin right here, wherever you are. If you're finding it hard to create and manage a daily practice, it's likely that you're making excuses when all you really need to do is to show up.

What's preventing you? Good intentions; according to the old saying, pave the road to hell. It's not enough to want or need to get things done. The only way to achieve your goals is to act on them.

Create a daily practice. When you set aside time each day for your ideas to flow, things begin to move forward. Understand your limitations and work with them by limiting distractions. Choose a quiet place that supports the routine. Boredom will soon be replaced by satisfaction when you see how enjoyable it is to meet your challenges. Wake up your motivation and step into your authentic life.

We are all born curious but seem to lose it over time. Humans teach children to block their natural inquisitive nature because the endless questions they ask are embarrassing. They are scolded, admonished. Shut up. Sit down. Stop staring. Behave. It's rude to ask questions.

Personally, I have an almost overwhelming need to understand what's going on in order to move forward with whatever knowledge I can glean from a situation. Sorry, not sorry. Asking questions is a perfectly logical way of discerning information and weighing outcomes. If we lose our ability to question things, we also give up understanding and empathy in any relationship we have with ourselves and others. Imagination is a big part of the ability to feel into another person's life. We absolutely need it to connect to each other.

Everyone has an infinite capacity for change. We are grounded by an intuitive logic that we can summon at any time to free us from negative thoughts and anger. Uncertainty is part of the human experience as well. Even if we don't completely understand what someone is going through, we can let them know that we are there for them just by showing up. Words are not always necessary. A simple hug can have a massively beneficial impact. Being available to nurture without judging or assuming is a positive way to care and express love.

Notice your feelings. Observe when you are upset or angry and try replacing those negative thoughts with curiosity. Question why you are experiencing this. Could you try to look at yourself differently, in a more nonjudgmental way? Looking inward to explore your own behavior is an indication of how you show tolerance in the way you view others. Finding new ways to accept and love yourself promotes mindfulness and awareness in all relationships. You can change your view of any situation by approaching it with your natural gift of curiosity. Ask the cat. It's satisfying.

Love yourself. Forgive yourself. Be true to yourself. How you treat yourself sets the standard for how others will treat you.

—**Steve Maraboli**

Have We Lost Our Mojo?/
People Have A Need To Talk
And We Need To Listen

It's hard to stay above the fray when everything you see or hear is depressing. We long for the day when we can leave home again to do things we once enjoyed without fear or worry.

At this moment in time when our spirits are so low, joy feels out of reach. There seems to be no end to the darkness that penetrates our positivity.

This is a sadness without borders, a deep wound that requires much care and nurturing. To shift the world and ourselves to a place of acceptance and compassion for each other, we need to communicate. Talk becomes conversation, conversation becomes action, action becomes accomplishment. It's a huge effort that will take time and humanity to make a difference and reconcile differences. If we open ourselves to compromise and forgiveness, we heal.

One drop of water is nearly invisible, but many drops of water fill an ocean. Banding together in solidarity is the only way to move forward from past injustices. Where will you add your drop of water? When a family member, friend, or co-worker is experiencing a stressful time, are we 100% available to reassure them that they are not alone? Or are we too busy managing or avoiding our own problems?

There are so many things that cause tension and strain for us. And they're universal.

Basic ones such as getting along with people at home or at work consume us daily. Money pressures—how to make more, spend less, pay bills, save for the future. Fear of illness or death is more pervasive than ever.

With many families huddled together in cramped quarters of late, we are constantly working on daily relationships. Some can be resolved easily by discussing them with friends, family, partners, or the people involved. Others are more serious and require a lot of introspection and counseling just to move forward. There is no such thing as closure when someone you love is gravely injured or dies.

Whenever your world changes in an unexpected way, sadness is rampant and too often hopelessness ensues. It is more than likely that everyone we love will suffer the loss of someone important to them at some point. We need to be available to listen to the people who come to us in pain. Even if we don't quite know what to say, we can offer them comfort just by listening. If someone you know needs compassion, open your arms and your heart. Small gestures are so meaningful at a time when a friend is hurting. Anything you do for those feeling isolated and alone is a gift to them. Even if they don't want to share their raw feelings, an offer of your time or an invite to a social distancing event may be welcomed.

We tend to stay away from people who've suffered a loss or are in pain because we don't know what to say or do. Let's remember the healing power of reaching out to each other. Let's listen without judgement. Let's hear with our hearts and offer love.

The I Ching says, "All life is interconnected. Everyone is one."

Dear Lost Boys, See Ya! Love, Peter/Where Does The Time Go?

Suddenly, freedoms that were oh so fun when you were younger become less delightful now that you have responsibilities. It's hard to keep a 9–5 job when you have been out all night drinking tequila shots with your buds. While it does suck not to have the youthful luxury to burn the midnight oil and sleep all day, you get to make cool choices like not living at home with your parents. You can pick a career because it's creative, or one that pays a lot of money. Or both. Either way, at a certain point, you decide to begin the adventurous journey to self-realization.

How did it happen? Maybe not as suddenly as you thought. You've been preparing even if you didn't know it. Be honest with yourself. You definitely don't have the same zest for the wild and crazy life as you once did. In the back of your mind, you were silently acknowledging that change was imminent and maybe welcomed. It's a huge seismic shift—the time to build a foundation for a new adult life.

Working to earn the money you need to pay bills requires leaving some of your previous pleasures behind. Accepting a new pattern of behavior for yourself and others may cause a few friendships to dissolve. That's a part of your journey. Evolution is a kind of divine intervention. Not everything needs to stay the way it once was. Trust the universe to have your back.

The rewards of growing up are too numerous to mention. Having the confidence to move forward and live an authentic life is the best opportunity you can give yourself and a positive sign of healthy well-being. You deserve a full and happy experience on this earth.

A routine is nothing more than making your mind up to do something and doing it. If you don't have time to get everything done, maybe you are just spending your time carelessly. Is it possible to shave an hour off the enjoyable rabbit hole of social media or television relaxation? How about two? Examine your activities. Write down your goals and track your progress. If the change seems harsh, consider how much you want to accomplish your stated goals.

Creating and following a routine involves choices and discipline. The upside is the satisfaction you experience when your goals are met. You will find you are empowered by the discovery of a newfound ability to act on tasks you have always wanted to do. Setting life goals is a way of honoring yourself. It helps you to process and keep your skills sharp to embrace new ways of learning. When the mind is occupied, the risk of depression is decreased. You become more patient in response to daily frustrations and unexpected changes. Remind yourself that you are taking important steps toward your future one day at a time, and take pride in your achievements.

As a healthy human, it's important to accept the inevitable possibility that not everything will happen as smoothly as you hope. Don't look at this as failure. Be ready to accept that unforeseen events derail even the best laid plans. So what? The only thing that matters is that you can get up and shake it off. It's not a reason to give up. It's a reminder that you are focused and forward moving.

even

in the loneliest moments

i have been there

for myself.

—**Sanober Khan**

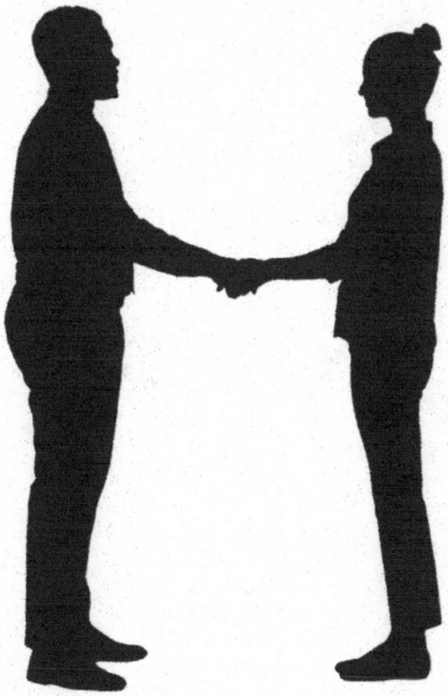

It's Not You, It's Me/Can We Talk?

Have you ever wondered why some people come into your life? One day you're thick as thieves and then suddenly the friendship is gone with the wind, leaving you to consider the brutal aftermath. Get used to it. Throughout life, people will come and go.

From social interactions to school, neighbors, work, internet dating, etc., we choose people with whom we can share experiences. Sometimes it's people we work with, neighbors, or others with whom we have found a common interest. Starting with kindergarten, where we form our first friendships, we begin pulling friends into our tribe. At first, it is more by location than choice. As we mature, our interests change and we choose friends differently. The revolving door of personal evolution naturally balances applicants.

Some friendships fall into the drive-by category. They come in burning hot for a very short time before flaming out completely. They're usually fun while they last. Usually.

Other people may be an important part of your life for many years. The top tier is the handful of rare friends who seem more like family than your actual family. Hold on tight to those.

Life is a game of give and take. Every single person you interact with is going to bring something. You are going to give them something back. Whether you're the teacher or the student, you both gain valuable knowledge from the sole experience of interacting with each other. After certain relationships, especially if it's an unpleasant or difficult one, you might choose not to stay in each other's lives. It came into your viewfinder for a reason. It's up to you to decide whether to accept an opportunity or sidestep a challenge.

Can we talk? No, seriously; *can* we or is it a lost art? I read every day about energy vampires, drainers, and friends, who suck all the air out of the room, etc., etc. What I don't see anymore is conversations without cell phones, FaceTime, or visual aids of some sort. Are we over-scheduled, overworked, over everything? Did we forget how much fun it is to share experiences with each other in that moment that will never come again? Must we continually update and document the minutiae of everyday life? Who actually cares about the foods we are eating or the places we are meeting? Maybe your mother. When was the last time you listened to a friend with genuine concern? Was it more recently than the last time you posted perfectly curated pictures with hashtags? Back to the not so long-ago days, people ate together at a table, looked into each other's eyes, and had a give-and-take flow of words. Maybe even animated or heated. Perhaps we felt free to speak without offending someone or being trolled or recorded. We could be honest, authentic, real. No one needed to grab center stage and post a photo. It was fun to be there.

Sometimes I see photos on the Internet of an event I've attended, where people look like they're having the best time ever. I only saw people snapping photos on camera phones of people who came alive the moment the camera appeared. The minute the camera stopped, the party did too. Did George Bernard Shaw see the future when he said, "The single biggest problem in communication is the illusion that it has taken place?" Put down your phone and ask a friend or a stranger a question and listen to their answer. It could change your life.

Ghostbusters/Pick Me!

Whether you're the ghoster or the ghostee, ghosting is a painful situation.

As the ghosted one, it's especially horrible if you suffer from abandonment or self-esteem issues. But even if you're full of confidence, an unexpected paradigm shift like this is difficult to recover from. It creeps up without warning as sudden communication and behavior changes invade a seemingly working relationship. It can happen in any and all connections with others.

Those cute little habits you previously loved are now annoying as hell. Or you desperately need a friend's full attention, and all they want to talk about is their amazing boyfriend . . . again. When you know that in a few days, the phone will ring because they want to talk about their horrible boyfriend . . . again. I'm not against venting. Listening is what friends do. It's healthy to be present for each other, but when it gets to the point where your friend is repeating the same behaviors without being solution-oriented or even realistic, it gets old, tiresome, and you just don't feel like listening anymore. Hence, the exit plan.

Ghosting can occur naturally. It's not always a disaster when it's reciprocal. Friends outgrow each other. You may begin to notice subtle changes in the way a person treats you, even if you pinky swore that you would be BFFs. What was interesting then is not so interesting now. Maybe you changed. Maybe they did. Either way, what drew you to each other so intensely is no longer something that holds you together. In a case like this, mutual distancing is acceptable. You've probably both been expecting it, so it might actually be a relief. Phone calls become less frequent, then disappear completely; there is an occasional text, a Facebook like or two, a Christmas card and then radio silence. Organic ghosting. No shade.

Keep in mind that ghosting is not the most acceptable or kind choice for the dissolution of a relationship. It speaks to who you are just as much as it does to the person you're trying to get away from. Their behavior might be something that mirrors things about you that you don't care for, and in that case, maybe the problem is with you and will take some introspection on your part. If possible, try to speak to the other person about what it is that is bothering you.

I've had friends who've talked with me about a behavior I wasn't aware I was exhibiting. Because they cared enough to come to me, I was able to make necessary changes to salvage our relationship. I've also spoken to friends who had no clue their judgmental words were hurting me. You have no idea what's going on in the mind of someone else. Sit at the peace table and have a heart-to-heart with the people who are important to you and move forward. If they are not open to it, a reassessment may be best for your mental health. At the very least, you've addressed it, which is what friends do when they care.

When you know your own value, you pick people who mirror that back to you.

Check your self-esteem: Do you apologize for decisions because you feel defensive about your choices? Are the people in your life taking advantage of you? Do you feel good about the friends you have? Are you negative? Consider this: You may be attracting the wrong people with your attitude. If so, your ego needs a reset. Look at yourself objectively. Be realistic about who you are, and determine what you require from a relationship. People treat you the way you let them. Rushing into a friendship negates the importance of making authentic and good choices.

If finding real friends doesn't happen quickly, take comfort in your own company. Being alone shouldn't bring on a panic attack. It's worth the patience and compassion necessary to choose the kind of people who lift you up, not the ones who hold you down. Give yourself the respect you deserve.

Obstacles Are Opportunities Waiting To Happen/If Wishes Were Horses, Beggars Would Ride

The Rolling Stones told us quite clearly that you can't always get what you want, but sometimes you get what you need. How we manifest our wishes influences their outcome. Maybe what we want is something we don't have, like money or a satisfying job, relationship or home. If we think about something constantly, does that mean we get it? Who doesn't want more, even if they have enough? Being aware of thoughts engages possibilities. Acting on them brings fruition.

If we make a passive wish, the chances of luck making it fall into our laps is pretty unlikely. If we act on our goals with a specific plan, the odds are in our favor. Small steps unlock unseen opportunities. An ability to adjust allows flexibility and growth. If you make a mistake along the way, moving methodically will save you from failure because you can learn from it. Balance is maintained with listening to your instincts and taking time to understand the best way forward.

A simple way to accomplish your goals successfully is to work for a company in the field that you intend to master. Honing your skills while moving toward your dream can help you reach it, especially if you are open to benefitting from any obstacles you come across on the apprenticeship. When something doesn't go as expected, look at the situation as a part of a process you need to master in the art of resolution. Putting time and effort into a task is necessary to achieve desired results.

If you believe your wish will be granted, you are already using your power to manifest its happening. Choose to start each day with a positive affirmation and attitude. Throw your coin into the fountain and pursue your dreams. Would you be surprised to know that the best day of your life hasn't even happened yet? So, while you have already accumulated a collection of magnificent days, you still have a lot more to look forward to!

It's good to remember when you are going through a difficult time that the temporary setback is merely a stone in your path. When you're able to look at the lesson that life is teaching you in those instances, you learn something useful about yourself. Try shifting your point of view to see how the most stressful times can lead to a new understanding of who you are. The growth you experience is proof that change is positive and always an option if you are ready to embrace it. Life happens quickly. Be ready. Kick the stone out of your path and keep moving.

Everything in the world is improved with an attitude of openness. If a choice becomes a challenge, consider the way you approach it. When you weigh an outcome without judgement, you can handle anything in life with clarity, compassion, and patience. If you're having issues at work or home, try organizing your thoughts before speaking. Plan a calm conversation with the other party instead. No matter how hard it is to have that talk, it's the way to seek resolution and harmony.

Opportunities are all around you. Use your inner toolbox to show you how they can assist in your quest to uncover the whole, healthy, and authentic person you were born to be.

Empathy/Apocalypse Now

First of all, what exactly is empathy? We think it's wondering how we would feel or react in the same situation. We think it's helping fix a problem, giving advice, or consoling someone. Guess what? It's none of those things. Empathy is presence.

When someone tells us about their situation, we look at our own experiences as if we were in their shoes. That's limiting though, because how we would feel or react or think really hasn't got anything to do with other people. Has anyone ever told you that they know how you feel? Since they can't access the inner workings of your mind, they can't possibly have a clue. It's the same as trying to figure out what it's like to be without hearing or eyesight. We have no idea, so instead of imagining, we are merely reflecting our own idea of what that experience would be like.

When I'm feeling low, I don't really want someone to tell me to "cheer up," or that "tomorrow is another day," and especially, "don't worry about it." I'm legit feeling bad and telling me to cheer up sounds like you're not paying attention to my feelings. I know that tomorrow is another day, but today, right now, I am worried. If you truly want to show empathy to someone, you have to take it outside of yourself. Just being there in that moment with them, feeling into their experience is powerful. You don't need to solve the problem. You might not be able to anyway, but if you are there sitting with them in their time of conflict or sadness, you might even connect to your own pain.

Being present has a way of radiating both outward and inward. Emphatically listening to someone doesn't involve any further participation than giving them your full attention. Even if you don't agree with their choices, you can listen and respect whatever they say with no judgement or attempt to fix it. Not only does it allow someone to be exactly who they are, they feel heard and understood.

Powerful.

I just got off a call with a friend who has owned a family restaurant in the East Village for 30 years. Since Covid-19, his peaceful and thriving neighborhood is now a dystopian landscape. Bustling restaurants are shuttered, or limited to a small area of outdoor seating. The subway closes each night for cleaning, displacing the usual denizens who ride the trains because they have nowhere else to go. Aggressive people roam the streets, shouting and sometimes even attacking unsuspecting diners. Coveted sidewalk tables, long a ritual of summer date nights, are another casualty of the recent pandemic. The only way small businesses can survive is if they are able to stay open. But how can they continue to exist when looming anarchy is quickly becoming a reality?

As my friend related his worries and fears for the future, I envisioned the bleak scenario he painted. It was almost impossible to imagine this metropolis, so different from the city I have known and loved for many years. Now that social distancing has become the norm, our humanity is threatened. We are losing the ability to share experiences with others. Daily stresses and struggles have made it hard to remain positive. It is ever more important to be aware and ready to diffuse a potential crisis.

When someone is pushing your boundaries, you may need to express anger. A stern message can remind them to back off, and possibly shift the situation. However, if you feel compromised or in danger, leave immediately or call for help. Likewise, if you notice someone having minor difficulty, you may be able to offer some assistance. Perhaps a small gesture, like a glass of water or a hand to carry a heavy package would be welcomed. Your seat on the bus. One kind word could be enough encouragement to help redirect their emotional struggle. Make their day. It will make yours.

Instead of judging, observe the scene before you act. Read the circumstances intuitively and choose to be empathetic in the way you relate to another person. Body language is a good way to communicate intent. Showing vulnerability communicates your humanity and signals compassion for frustration. Humans can weather any storm if we work together. Let's cultivate the present and manifest our future.

The Past/Leave The Past In The Past

When you look back at your past honestly and assess what has happened in your life, you will begin to realize that there are many dimensions to your actions. Being hard on yourself is unfair. Choosing to deal with your feelings positively through forgiveness gives you the ability to see your life through the lens of compassion. Your free will allows you to move forward whenever you are ready. Only through forgiving yourself can you truly heal any resentment you have about your past.

Let it go!

Some things just are. They happen whether you want them to or not. How do you go with the flow? You resist the temptation to get annoyed. Instead, close your eyes and breathe deeply and slowly. It will immediately elevate your mood. Giving up the need to control allows you to be open in ways you may not even imagine. Why preclude possibilities? When you allow yourself to experience all of your emotions, you can sort out feelings and reactions to old conflicts in situations. Re-examining the past will enable you to heal and move forward comfortably.

If you want to see your future, look at your past. If you want to change your life, accept your past. Whatever your past has been is an accurate prediction of what your future will be. When the desire to change your life is stronger than continuing the same cycle of pain and core beliefs, your future will be transformed. Let go of beliefs that no longer serve you.

Your first core beliefs were given to you by your parents. It's probable that you accepted them unconsciously and without question. As an adult, you have the power to reject old patterns and choose your own set of core beliefs that will better serve and elevate you. Until you do that, you'll be carrying around some often harmful and self-defeating judgements. Are you strong enough to separate old core beliefs and embrace new ones that will give you the self-esteem, freedom, and ability to move forward?

I'd Love To, But I Wash My Hair On Tuesday Nights . . . /If You Don't Expect Too Much From Me, I Might Not Let You Down

Excuses. We all make them. Sometimes it's necessary. Maybe you don't want to hurt someone's feelings. That's a legit reason as far as I'm concerned.

But let's be brave and address the elephant in the room—the other kind of excuses that hold us back from moving forward. We use them to thwart any thought of reasonable solution when we don't want to do it, didn't do it, or won't do it.

Blame it on the difficult daily decisions you are forced to make: prioritizing work, children, friends, and relatives. All your choices figure into the oh so valid reasons why things just don't get done. Not to mention phone calls, texting, and other distractions. And don't forget the time spent watching TV and surfing the Internet. How can we possibly enjoy the good life without these small mercies? We don't have to.

Create a schedule that allows time for everything on your list. A balanced program can prioritize the hours spent on each task or activity so that everything fits neatly in. Sure, maybe you can't play Rocket League for two hours, but you can block off 30 minutes a day on the roster for gaming and still have time to do kitchen chores and work assignments. It's not verboten if it's written into your agenda. When you get into the rhythm of an organized plan, movement forward becomes as easy as breathing. It feels good to tick off tasks on your list.

Remember, you only need to challenge yourself. Your true friends will be supportive when you let them know you're working toward a goal. If they're not, maybe you should reevaluate the friendship. Be positive. All you need to do is to decide to do it. If you mess up, do it again. Don't waste time punishing yourself. It's a learning curve. If you don't know how to do something, consult the oracle (Google). There are lots of short how-to videos for anything you can think of. You can even unblock a toilet without a plunger, who knew (I do now)! Take a class, read a book, educate yourself. It's exciting to learn something, and you can tell other people about your newly acquired skills the next time you get together. You may even inspire someone.

We all have expectations. Sometimes it's hard to know the difference between the world in your head and the outer world. Therapist Jean Piaget referred to this as "magical thinking." He believed we outgrow it by age seven. The Law of Attraction touts the belief that we can attract events into our lives by just thinking about them. The thought alone can give us happiness. But what happens when our expectations involve other people? Why are we upset, even resentful, if our expectations of someone are not met? The ensuing disappointment that occurs when things don't turn out the way we expect them to feels awful.

It's unreasonable to assume people will make the same choices you do. If your expectations are unspoken, the probability of them being lived up to is slight. In other words, just because you do something for someone, there's no guarantee that you can expect it in return.

I once had a conversation with my brother, expressing disappointment in the way he behaved toward me. He told me to lower my expectations. I assured him that I had. He smiled and said: "not low enough." Let go of expectations. Even if things don't turn out the way you hoped, your takeaway won't be the one of resentment. No one is here to live up to your expectations, including you. It is what it is, and if things don't work out the way you would have liked, try being grateful for the lesson you learned from it. Every cloud has a silver lining.

Are You A Real Phony?/Have You Got A Secret?

In the 1961 film *Breakfast at Tiffany's,* Holly Golightly's agent asks her neighbor Paul to tell him whether he thinks Holly is real or phony. Paul says he doesn't know, and the agent responds, "You're right. She's a real phony. She honestly believes all this phony junk that she believes."

Suddenly, this makes a lot of sense to me. Because now I'm thinking about who we are in public and who we are in private and why it's so important to us to maintain a persona of perfection. In a world of filters, camera angles, and photoshop, we can seamlessly reinvent ourselves to get the acceptance we crave. We can edit and sanitize every detail.

We can redesign and broadcast this much more palatable version of ourselves into the world on our social media pages. No one has to know who we really are. We'll never have to show them the real us because this version is so much better. So, we conceal our anxieties, cover our imperfections, and create who we want the world to see and accept.

Are we the real phony? When you love yourself, you inspire others to do the same and your like-minded tribe will gather. Love the real you. You're amazing!

I see a life filled with wonder and dreams that come true in a utopian paradise where no one is hurt or sick. There is a bountiful table with delicious food for all. Everyone is happy and kind. Birds sing and flowers bloom. In my imagination, there is no discord. Wouldn't that be amazing . . . and then, I wake up. We need to begin each day with hope in our hearts. Everything changes and so will we.

Now that we are in the midst of unprecedented challenges, it's a chance to reset our personal goals and connections. It's a time to take inventory of the secrets we hold and the walls we erect. Coming to terms with your secrets and losing the fear of letting them go brings people together. Recovery from past traumas is possible when you confront them and the emotions that have held you down. Resentments that have no place in mental balance and self-care isolate you from social support and wellness. Fear and shame are unwelcome when you want to live an authentic life.

Your secrets are safer out than in. Release them. Give yourself the love you deserve with the positive affirmation that you are a perfectly imperfect human, just like everyone else.

Wearing The Hair Shirt/
Moving Forward

Are you the same person that you were ten years ago? Would you make the same choices now? Why are we so quick to judge mistakes that others have made in the past?

I have personally made many changes because of consequences, education, empathy, and/or a new understanding of life in general. In other words, I'm not the person I once was. I hope that I'm a better human now because of my mistakes. Should I still be judged by youth or ignorance when I have worked hard to move forward from my poor decisions? I own my responsibility in how badly my thoughtless choices damaged others and myself. The person I am now acknowledges that who I was then brought me here today. You may have been taught a code of values and behaviors as a child that don't reflect your own.

By calling forth your ability to understand the feelings of others, you can choose whether to embrace or reject that old blueprint. You can rewrite your pattern. I've watched people on the Internet apologizing for things they did or said years ago; children and adults who may not have known better at that time but have now owned their mistakes. They have moved on from that stagnant place, and their present choices reflect growth and humanity. They are no longer who they once were.

We are currently in an upheaval—a time of conflict and change in the world, and especially in our country. Call forth your ability to understand and remember that forgiveness is part of our human experience. Persecuting others is a way of hating ourselves. It doesn't further a bad situation to perpetrate it. Can we find it in our hearts to allow the folly of youth to be the reason they made those choices and appreciate their positive evolution? Let's forgive ourselves and others. Let's embrace love and compassion. As Oscar Wilde said, "Every saint has a past, and every sinner has a future."

We change our wants and needs as we move from childhood into adulthood—friends, food choices, activities, political views. As we begin to understand who we are, we start to hone in on who we want to be. This is when we make pivotal decisions about how we want to live our lives.

There are so many ways to open your mind to the infinite possibilities of an authentic life. A new perspective and attitude can color the way you judge others and yourself. Traveling teaches tolerance and patience by exposing you to different cultures and situations. Reading is another positive way to gain knowledge by discovering and exploring new ideas. It's also interesting to enhance your own experiences by seeing them through someone else's eyes. You may even be motivated to try a new skill that exposes a hidden talent.

Most of all, it's essential to feel comfortable with yourself. The way you let others treat you is influenced by the way you see yourself. Loving yourself for who you are both inside and out lets other like-minded people find you. When you learn the value of simply being you, you know who you are. You're on the journey to fulfillment.

I Don't Care If I'm Old, I Just Don't Want To Feel It!/All Around The Mulberry Bush

As we age, challenges become more difficult. There are so many unwelcome changes that it becomes hard to maintain a positive attitude during these transitions. Friends die, health becomes an issue, children move away, we retire (and in many cases, that brings boredom or anger from the loss of freedom). Our personal power is reduced or placated, rendering us unimportant and in the way. Simply refuse to accept the traditional definition of old.

The years you've lived have given you the wisdom to accept what you cannot change and the knowledge to explore your options carefully. So how can you regain independence and maintain wellness as you age? By choosing healthy foods, a regular program of exercise, social activity, and a strong mental attitude; managing stress is easier. When you reprogram your mind, you thrive. Face it, there are things you can't change.

You begin to have trouble participating in activities that were once easy, and there are a few you're not able to do at all. So what? Understand that it's essential to move slowly and appreciate your body for all it does to keep you upright and active. Value what you can do and find other ways to accomplish challenges, or just let them go. Not everything is important. It's easy to take things for granted . . . until they are gone. Notice the many small and amazing opportunities you have to be grateful for. Enjoy your morning coffee as you listen to the birds singing outside. Smiling yet?

Take action when a challenge confronts you, rather than ignoring it. Use it as an opportunity for personal growth instead. Your confidence will inspire you. The restriction placed on all of us by COVID-19 is a reminder to express gratitude whenever we can. Make an effort to process your feelings. It can be helpful to talk with others, meditate, or keep a journal. Better out than in, as Shrek said! I decided a long time ago that I didn't want to do anything that wasn't fun. While that may seem like a black-and-white choice, it's actually not hard if you let go of the silly notion that you don't deserve it. According to the Oxford Dictionary, fun is "amusement, especially lively or playful." The caveat? The activities you enjoy may not be fun for other people, and vice versa. Fun is subjective. I don't want to go cage swimming with sharks, but more than a few of my adventurous pals find it to be an exhilarating experience. Shudder. On the other hand, I think it's absolutely wonderful to spend hours sorting through button bins to find the perfect complement to my new jacket. I don't think it's surprising to imagine that I share this passion with pretty much no one else.

Everyone can agree that fun is positive. Whenever humans share an experience with each other, it develops a bond that brings them together. It also helps reduce stress to do something that makes us laugh. An intense situation is decreased when we find the humor in it. A spontaneous burst of laughter kills a negative moment. I used to be annoyed when I lost my train of thought. Now I recognize that the rapid flood of ideas coming into my mind occasionally drowns my words. Big deal. It feels good to know that my brain is creative and engaged. If you're feeling out of balance, try moving a bit. A silly dance, a workout session, or a walk can elevate your hormone levels and mood. If you put it into your daily routine, you'll continue to reap the benefits of the fun it brings you. The moment you feel a bit deflated or low, go online and participate in a group exercise or dance. You may even laugh at yourself, which is the most fun of all.

Taking yourself too seriously invites anxiety and depression. Enjoy the small pleasures of energetic physical movement. It's way more entertaining to be amused rather than deflated. Laughter is the antidote to overthinking and stress. So, why be serious? Pop goes the weasel!

An Argument Is Like A Pancake: It Has Two Sides/Let Me Talk!

Humans need all their emotions. We don't always have control over our feelings, so resolution is necessary in those moments. Ignoring or venting anger is an unhealthy choice that promotes inner resentment and anxiety. Fearing confrontation or feeling the need to be in control breeds bitterness.

There is often a better outcome if you pause to consider your options. It is unproductive and harmful to silently seethe or react negatively instead of trying to find a compromise. Loud voices signal a warning threat of danger, making it hard to hear an argument logically, no matter how sound it is. Understanding is blocked when someone shouts or lashes out physically. It can quickly escalate into a destructive emotional battle with each side becoming defensive. If substance abuse is a part of the behavior, it needs to be addressed separately with empathy and may take professional evaluation to aid in recovery.

What are you really angry about? Identify what triggers you and find a positive way to shift your response. Choosing to be open and solution-oriented in dealing with a situation is the best-case scenario. Patience helps when your temperature is rising and you feel anger bubbling. Think about what you need to say before you speak. Take a deep breath and count to ten. How important is it? Is it really worth getting angry and ruining your day? Anger doesn't have to be violent or abusive. It's actually a normal and useful emotion when the message conveyed is properly addressed. Using compassion to assert yourself is a healthy way to be angry. Consider whether it's more important to be right or to resolve.

Being humble is a magnificent thing. It allows you to be aware, open to another point of view, and show concern for others besides yourself. How can we have a discussion without it turning into a confrontation? Leave judgement out of it. In this crazy world chaos, it seems we have forgotten how to be humble enough to set aside our egos. More than ever, people have very different points of view and need to reinforce the way they see the world in their own way. Close-mindedness takes a toll on relationships in every arena. Is it so important to be right? If you don't like the way a conversation is going, try not to view it defensively or with anger. Maybe it's actually a teachable moment and you can learn, or at the very least understand that it's ok to disagree.

Use your ability to let the person speak their mind, even if you think your approach is more effective. They may not want to hear it. Be empathetic to their need to unload and quietly listen. Sometimes a few moments of venting are all it takes. It probably has nothing to do with you, but if it does, it's more important to resolve than to be right. If you can help someone find clarity just by listening to them, why not? Being concerned doesn't always require a response to their dilemma. Take the focus off yourself and connect with whatever the real need of that person is.

One of my friends told me that when she'd tell her boyfriend about frustrations with a co-worker, he would attempt to resolve the situation by offering solutions. She finally said to him, "Please listen and don't keep trying to fix it. I just have to say it. If it's boring, think about your golf game. I won't even notice." In the end, she realized that telling her girlfriends was a much more a satisfying experience. How wonderful to hear an echo of what she was thinking: "Ugh. What a jerk. He's ridiculous." She didn't need resolution from anyone, she just wanted someone to listen. And that's all it took to make her feel better.

That's Not My Pig!/The Fifth Circle Of Hell

Because if it were your pig, you'd never let it destroy your beautiful farm, would you? Harboring resentment, holding on to old hurts, and replaying unresolved conversations or judgements do not serve you in the here and now. All the time you spend rewriting the would-haves, should-haves, and could-haves, wastes valuable mental energy that your brain could use way more productively. Why let messy thoughts roam around wildly and cause havoc in your head? You may never get the resolution or understanding that you fantasize about because you have zero control over what other people say or do.

What you can control is your reaction and response to situations that don't deserve your focus. Unless you think an honest discussion can bring about resolution, it's not important enough to allow negativity to nestle in your mind rent free. Let it go. Your farm will be so much calmer if you evict the pig that causes the mayhem.

Examine the feelings it stirs up when you think about what happened. Then consider whether the people who caused it even remember the incident that you've been reliving, possibly for years. I will venture to guess they never gave it a second thought. Meanwhile, you've allowed it to destroy your farm. Get the shovel and clean out the pigpen. I guarantee you'll be happier once you let go of that ornery pig who's crashing there. You could foster a sweet baby goat instead. Much more satisfying.

I am sitting outside peacefully, watching hummingbirds play with each other on the red flowered bushes when I feel it. Red hot dripping rage. My wandering mind has tripped a landmine in my closet of memories and there it is. Boom! I hear my late father's voice in my ear: "Anger is your favorite emotion." A declaration. A rhetorical statement that requires no response.

My inner child has a question: Why didn't you ask me why I was so angry? My adult self has the answer: Because you didn't want to know. Because you already knew. Because you didn't want to take responsibility for the choices you made that put me in harm's way. Holding on to anger is like drinking poison and expecting the other person to die. I have survived those dark days of childhood, but in order to fully let go of the resentment I harbor, I need to erase my father's judgmental words to thrive and heal.

Morning the loss and neglect of your inner child is not the same as feeling sorry for yourself. Mine needs comfort and compassion to move forward. She doesn't need to be rescued. She needs to be heard and honored to be set free. I acknowledge my right to experience and feel each of my emotions. Old judgements won't hold me prisoner when I am no longer shackled to an outdated pattern that I didn't choose.

Vulnerability/How's The Weather By You?

How you bond with others is the key to all of your relationships. It's important to know who you are before you're able to successfully connect with other humans. The essential exploration of your expectations begins with awareness of your own emotions, hopes, dreams, goals and fears. Determine realistic goals by thoroughly studying the risks and rewards of undertaking them. Will you truly be able to achieve a particular outcome you've chosen? Be honest with yourself. That being said, setting a comfortable goal that is likely to happen can sometimes be a way of avoiding rejection and disappointment.

Being cautious is often a go-to option to bypass pain. Why not occasionally try an uncomfortable way to confront fear? Whenever you divert from a usual solution, it stretches your development and growth in new ways. You may find the panic that you harbor disappears. Always going with safe and predictable options holds you back from exploring exciting possibilities. It blocks your natural spontaneity. Sure, it may be the easiest choice, but is that actually who you are now? Maybe it's just an old pattern you need to rewrite.

When contemplating an option, it is important to consider how it affects others. Examine a few different alternatives to decide whether it will hurt or offend anyone or make you feel bad, careless, or unkind. Doing the right thing should be intuitive, but sometimes it's just not. Speak your mind with the same perimeters. What is the best way to say what you mean without dumping negativity on another person? It's polarizing and unnecessary to cause discomfort to anyone. Are you mirroring a trait you don't care for in yourself?

Expect the road on your journey to sometimes meander off the beaten path of predictability. That's one of the most beautiful perks of being human. It is perfectly fine to be vulnerable, as long as you expect that sharing your emotions will occasionally take you down an uncharted and serendipitous path to self-discovery.

A lot of friendships are based on an unstable foundation, especially of late, when conversations remain at surface level. It seems we don't know what to talk about besides the horrors of coronavirus and the pervasive anxiety that's permeating the world. Sure, we might break it up occasionally with a bit of gossip about the Kardashians or our neighbors, but what has happened to discussing things we actually care about, or how we're doing? If you want to have a real relationship with someone, you have to be able to be honest without fear of judgement.

It's hard to achieve intimacy in a relationship when all we discuss is politics, sports, or the weather. Of course, everyone's worried about each other. Talking about it gives us a break from thinking about our own anxiety. But what if what we're pointing out in a family member or friend is something we're anxious about in ourselves? Do couples talk about their children so that they don't have to talk about other subjects that make them feel defensive? Mirroring is a way of shifting inner anxiety away from ourselves. It doesn't make it go away. In fact, it has a polarizing effect.

How do you develop a relationship with another person? Start by sharing something more personal instead of the kind of chatter that furthers superficial connection. Nobody wants to feel awkward in a relationship, but if you don't go deeper, you will miss having a more satisfying and intimate link.

Beginning with your family, consider the possibility that you choose benign or impersonal topics so that you don't have to talk about things that might be inflammatory or difficult. Perhaps telling another person something interesting about yourself will inspire them to let their own defenses down. True openness is essential to laying a successful foundation. Achieving a deeper experience requires an honest connection with ourselves and others.

Practical Magic/Self-Esteem

Good news:

The universe has gifted you with intuition.

Caveat:

It doesn't mean you're a prophet. What it does mean is that you possess the ability to invite change into your life just by using your inner toolbox. It is essential to the "here and now" to review and understand how you arrived at this moment.

Discovering who you are and what you need to do to achieve your goals requires reflection and determination. You ready? Taking risks or acting on instinct is a way of tapping into and listening to your intuition. It may feel uncomfortable or intense. That's entirely human response to the perception of conflict. Embrace the idea that the knowledge which comes from any action you take is worthwhile.

Your past has a way of hanging around, nudging and signaling you to consider opportunity or change. You may think it's comfortable, but being stuck actually creates more anxiety. Why not use your innate personal power to reflect and review that decision? You'll wonder what took you so long. When you suffer from low self-esteem, impulses are often frightening and restrictive. Summon the courage to believe in your choices to guide you and follow through with action. Even if a situation seems difficult in that particular moment, it is an opportunity to move forward in a new direction. Every option offers a chance for growth. Intuition is not a Ouija board or a crystal ball. It's already in you. You don't need to do anything other than be open and listen to it. Recharge your life with determination and love for yourself. I see a bright future ahead . . .

Self-esteem defines who you are through the acceptance of responsibility for your own empowerment. It gives you courage and ability to separate from the crowd and stand in your own truth. When you believe in your decisions, you are able to move forward without fear of judgement from others. Your inner strength will guide you to truly understand how you feel in a situation. If your gut is signaling information, pay close attention. Engage your mind to decipher the message you're receiving and decide if it furthers or hinders your development.

Once you've realized that your opinions are valuable and worthy of respect, you'll hear your authentic voice clearly. People's values may have some influence over your choices positively or negatively, but a powerful belief in yourself allows for introspection and careful reflection of their advice or warnings. It requires maturity to be aware and genuine in oneself. This important recognition is the first of many lessons along the human journey.

Continue to ask yourself questions to promote your education for solutions in problem-solving, then use intuition to sort through feelings and circumstances. Maintain focus on your goals and the path you've chosen. This is the only way to reach genuine resolution and love. If you know who you are, no one can tell you who to be. Connection to yourself is the most important relationship you'll ever have. It defines every relationship you'll ever have with others.

Our Collective Epiphany/ Positive Lens

Have you ever experienced an epiphany?

Many people have had a sudden change in direction because of something unexpected they saw, felt, or discovered. Recent events have given us reason to question everything. The world has shifted in a way we could never have imagined.

The coronavirus pandemic, quickly followed by consecutive racially charged issues, has made us painfully aware of our lack of humanity and hurtful inequality. Past choices are no longer acceptable nor humane. The ensuing upheaval and revolution have forced us to revisit and redefine our history and our future. We need to understand the part of our history that has brought us to this moment. The only way to move forward is together, in solidarity and love.

Each day when you wake up, you have a choice of how you view the world. It can be difficult to have a positive attitude with so many recent limitations and restrictions, but your perspective is the key to your happiness. I like to meditate in the morning as a way to welcome in and honor every experience that comes to me. While we don't have control over everything, we can decide how we respond in situations, even if they are frustrating or difficult. This time in history is only a setback if you look at it that way. Why not see it as a way to take a step back instead? Viewing life through a positive lens constructively redirects an experience.

Often, what we think we want is not what we actually need. A rejection could be a blessing if you consider how it affected you. If you learned from it, you gained wisdom. If you felt bad about it, you chose shame. Although you can't change what you did, you can choose to change your reaction to it. Focusing on the beauty in the world brings joy to you and everyone you encounter.

Manifesting Your Power/
Seek Discomfort

What if you suddenly realize the path you're on is not really your own? First, question everything. Second, challenge your choices or the choices that were influenced or chosen by a parent or teacher. Then decide to stop being afraid of failure or disappointment.

Change the way that you speak to yourself from negative to positive.

Instead of asking yourself if you will fail, tell yourself that you will succeed. Make a conscious decision that happiness is more important than fear. Believe in yourself. Once you open your true self, your healing begins. Write all unfulfilled goals on a piece of paper or in your journal. Don't think too much, just let them come out. Then go back and question each of them. Is the belief a fact or a judgement? Judgements that you or someone else made on you are blockages that hold you back from fulfilling your dreams.

Let go of anxiety that negates possibilities. Make a real commitment to yourself. It takes action to make change, and planning is necessary for success. If you want to lose weight, design a simple program that you can follow and keep daily track of your progress. If you want a different job, rewrite your resume to reflect and highlight your qualifications. Educate yourself with online courses. Read books. Talk to people. There are so many ways you can move forward and achieve everything you want.

Be honest with yourself, set small goals, and keep your word. You're either doing it or you're not. There's no gray area. Your continued commitment is a guarantee for your success. Seek discomfort to remind yourself that the only way to grow is to do things that make you uncomfortable. It's often hard to accept change, and made worse when forced upon you.

But as my dear friend Auguste Garufi says, something good always comes out of everything.

So where is the good in the pandemic? Everywhere. People are coming out of themselves to help others in ways even they never thought of before. We are rediscovering and reinventing ourselves with new choices. We are shifting forward despite the many roadblocks.

The power of every experience you have with others, no matter how simple, can cause a reflection of thought or behavior. Maybe it inspires or changes their thinking. Maybe it changes your thinking. Problems are only able to trigger feelings of insecurity, shame, envy, or revenge if we deny that they are part of us. Being overcome by such feelings forces us to recognize and consciously integrate them as natural parts of our psyche.

To develop a loving acceptance of ourselves and others, we need to see answers to our questions and solutions to our problems by working together. All of our past experiences continue to accompany us throughout our lives and considerably affect the way we feel today. Profound changes and even healing experiences are possible, although sometimes unsettling and hectic. If you can stay calm and allow things to happen without putting up too much resistance, you will feel a noticeable sense of relief. This is because just about everything now happening can help to increase your inner integrity. Seek discomfort to find comfort.

Collateral Damage/Ride Or Die

It's not possible to move forward unless you're willing to look back. Sometimes, what we need to learn comes from previous experiences that caused pain or seemed judgmental. Shift your view to accept that the hardest lessons are actually valuable blessings, nourishing both mind and spirit. Our most difficult relationships teach empathy, patience, and compassion. Once you look at your life honestly, you can release all negativity, realizing that all life experiences bring humans the gift of understanding and growth.

The people you have chosen as friends may need to be part of your examination as well. Not everyone you meet is going to be in your life forever. Some will be there for a long time, others not. Then there are the rare ride-or-die comrades that you have for life. It's always comforting to know someone whom you can count on to show up for you anywhere, anytime, if you need them. Once in a while, take inventory of the people you've chosen. Are they there for you, or just there? It isn't always easy, but when you assess your tribe with clarity, you will recognize the signs of the emotional vampires. It's exhausting to shoulder the weight of people who don't stand in their own truth.

A teacher of mine told me that carrying other people's burdens is like having a pocket full of stones as you walk up a hill. They weigh you down and make it harder to get to your destination. Leave the stones behind. When choosing between yourself and someone else in a situation like this, always choose yourself. Listening to yourself is the healthiest way to understand.

Real friends love you despite the parts of you that are even hard for you to love. They think you're funny even when you're not, describe you as quirky instead of weird, and keep your deep secrets safe. Genuine homies wipe your tears when you cry over a lost romance (even if they hated them), or help you move out under the cover of darkness if necessary. Friends know when you need a caramel latte and a hug. They're on your side and in your corner through thick and thin. They don't ask questions you don't want to answer. They tell you things you need to hear.

True friends staunchly support you on a regular basis. They always have time for you and call or text to check in—not just when they need something from you. They're actually interested in what you're up to and will listen enthusiastically even if it's a bit boring. When you mess up, they understand and forgive you. You are always in their hearts, even if you are a continent away. It doesn't matter if you have one or a dozen special people who encourage you to explore new interests or ideas. In other words, accepting you unconditionally and without judgement is the measure of a real friend. What matters most is that they value and respect every bit of you.

The Curious Case Of Cancel Culture/Strength In Numbers

I apologize in advance if you are offended by what you are about to read. Please feel free to tell me your thoughts after you hear mine, and we can have a civilized discourse. I'm absolutely open to listening to your point of view.

I don't understand how public shaming grew to such mob mentality. When did we start taking everything so seriously? What happened to humor? What happened to agreeing to disagree? What happened to respect? But most of all, what happened to kindness? When I look back on the many different choices I've made throughout my life, there are some that still make me cringe. Luckily, social media wasn't a thing then, so there were no cameras and microphones to record my misdeeds and mistakes. Youth is for learning and figuring out who you are. As long as you follow the Golden Rule, you're bound to find your true self along the way to adulthood. Of course, choosing role models who exemplify good principles also helps to keep your path clear.

Regardless, there are times when you need to burn your finger to know that fire is hot, no matter how many times your parents warned you. I don't want to be censored for stating my honest opinion. You may not agree, and that's fine with me as long as you don't insist that I adopt your belief either. I may not agree with you, but I'm going to let you speak without interrupting. Maybe you will sway me or vice versa. Maybe not. We can still have a hug and a coffee afterwards. It's not going to destroy our friendship as long as we accept that each other's options are exactly that.

Lately, we've been putting everyone under the microscope, digging up old secrets and past behaviors that no longer define them. It's not fair. We need to be allowed to evolve. Why are we not encouraged rather than punished? I don't want to be defined by who I was in my teens or 20s. Is it our place to ostracize others or be intolerant of their views just because they don't fit in with ours? All words have weight, but some words are weapons. I believe in the kind of free speech that excludes discriminatory and derisive racism, sexism, and homophobia.

Let's embrace the willingness we need to understand and accept that the benign differences between us require tolerance. We don't have the right to cancel anyone simply because they don't share our credo. We do have the responsibility to renounce discrimination and negative judgements within ourselves. Hate keeps us apart when we most need love to bring us together. We are surrounded by violence and injustice whenever we turn on the television. We hear it in the streets and read it in the news. It's hard to know whether to speak out or remain silent when everything we do or say is a possible conflict or argument. More than ever, we need to actively and responsibly choose to bring about an atmosphere of peace, love, and calmness to the troubled world we inhabit.

The harsh climate enveloping us right now is not new. Every civilization has been affected by injustice and conquest. Throughout history, the desire for control and dominance has steadily created an atmosphere of greed and violence that is now escalating toward certain anarchy and annihilation of the entire human race. It grows stronger every time we turn our backs on the chance to embrace peaceful forward movement. Every progressive thought and feeling we foster has the potential to shake the foundation of chaos we created. Each of us can make a difference. We are powerful when we are healthy within ourselves, but unstoppable when we work together. We can create a more balanced model of thought and deed to bring compassion and understanding to our planet and ourselves.

Instead of continuing to close our eyes to hate and destruction, let's consciously begin a collective paradigm shift. The conflicts we are experiencing are a result of missed opportunities for resolution. If we see our differences as a reason to be open to the possibilities of shared enlightenment and growth, we can break the cycle of war and discontent. When we spread love, there are no fractions, no greater than or lesser than. There is one whole human race.

in·ter·loper *(noun)*/Letter To My 13-Year-Old Self

A person who becomes involved in a place or situation where they are not wanted or are considered not to belong.

Today, I was listening to David Bowie's *Starman* and thinking about how to respond to an email I received from a young girl. She told me the children at her school bully her because she looks and sounds different. Instead of welcoming her with the natural curiosity of childhood, their words are cruel and unkind. Ironically, her parents chose to leave the comfort of their own country, taking jobs well beneath their skill sets so that she could have a better life. I feel her sadness.

My son went to a Montessori school where children of all ages and backgrounds treated each other with respect and kindness. When he transferred to public school in fifth grade, he encountered bullying and hate from the other children. Because he hadn't grown up in the town, he was not welcomed. He never received an invitation to a party or activity. Their exclusion allowed him to develop skills and pursue projects that have led to his successful career. That harsh lesson was actually a blessing. He learned that he did not need their approval to feel good about himself. He knew who he was even if they didn't.

Children are not born with hate in their hearts. They are delicate sponges who absorb beliefs and language from their surroundings. Hate is a learned and divisive tool. It begins at home and covers the world like kudzu. What is happening in our country now is a result of many microcosms like these. Clearly, we need change, compassion, kindness, and resolution if we are going to survive. We need to love and show our children that love doesn't judge. We need to be present to listen and speak up. We need to celebrate our differences, not let them divide us. We need to be one world with one human race.

What would I tell my 13-year-old self? I would tell her to be patient because everything she's dreaming of is possible. I would express that kindness is not always reciprocated, but that should never stop her from being kind. I would say that expressing anger is human, feeling sadness is cathartic, and speaking her mind is necessary. I would remind her that bravery is sometimes a small act, sometimes not, but always valuable. I would encourage her to embrace change because it's always an option and a solution. But most of all, I would ask her to remember that being herself is perfectly lovely and quite enough, no matter what anyone tells her. Because if she knows who she is, no one can tell her who she should be.

Days Of Heaven/The Gratitude Habit

The tumultuous and polarizing sociopolitical upheaval of the world has transformed our normal existence in many extreme and uncomfortable ways. It's not hard to think it has changed us for the worse. The simple days of our grandparents with the guaranteed promise of a white picket fence and a chicken in every pot is a faded fairytale.

When life is so upended, it's natural to yearn for what we once took for granted. Remembering how things once were and reliving pleasant memories gives us hope for the future. It also reminds us that those times will never return. The unprecedented changes have threatened our stability, stopped us in our tracks, and restricted our freedoms. More than ever, we need to keep our loveliest reminiscences close. Looking back is a comforting way of re-experiencing unconditional love to help us to cope with the difficulties of the here and now.

Open your box of personal nostalgia to reassure yourself of better days ahead. It's therapeutic. These stored memories keep us present and moving forward. They hold the twilight rays of sadness and depression at bay, helping to connect us to ourselves and others.

Just when we started to get somewhat used to the unprecedented restrictions of COVID-19, the rules changed again. Services started to open up in places. Restaurants offered curbside pickup, barbers cut hair, retail stores delivered to your doorstep. Many small and large pleasures we had taken for granted in the past resumed. It began to feel hopeful again, as if an end to isolation was possible. But just as suddenly, being able to join each other caused a new kind of anxiety. Constant announcements bombarded television, radio, and social media, warning us to be vigilant. Wear your masks, social distance, and sanitize. Wash your hands. Don't touch your face. Now we have a new dilemma. Do we really want to leave the safety and security of home? It can be a frightening decision.

Dealing with stress is difficult, but even more so for people who haven't learned to enjoy their own time. Relying on others and a busy social schedule of activities is not possible right now. We have to use coping skills to get through this. At some point, this deadly virus will be a minor annoyance, like flu. But for now, it's up to each of us to find ways to move forward with positivity.

Start your day with a mental gratitude list. People you love, places you've visited, your sweet pet being silly. Remind yourself to smile by looking through photos or calling someone you miss. Write in your journal. Paint. Purge your closet. Watch the squirrels play outside your kitchen window. It's up to you to rediscover the joy in every one of your precious moments. Replace fear with appreciation and compassion for the world. Feeling grateful for things both big and small is an excellent way to honor yourself and hold love in your heart.

We accept the love we think we deserve.

—Stephen Chbosky

Your Inner Child/Breaking The Chains

Your past has a firm influence on who you are right now. In order to move forward, you need to learn how to love and embrace every part of you. Your personal history and environment influences and stores memories along with their positive and negative impact.

Every experience you have from the time you were born is blueprinted first by family and later reinforced by friends, relatives, teachers, and anyone else you encounter once you go out into the world. It's up to you to revisit those experiences and decide for yourself if you should keep them in your happy place or view them as lessons to move forward. You can look at all the events in your life positively because no matter what had happened in the past, it brought you here today. By shifting your perspective toward self-love and acceptance, healing begins.

Negative thoughts are often overwhelming, causing low self-esteem and imbalances. Issues of this kind can spiral and result in poor decisions that are based on a general lack of trust in oneself. People go to great lengths to discover why they have these behaviors and how to address them constructively. It can be a lifelong journey to understand and heal. The more people you meet, the more you realize that there is no such thing as a perfect childhood.

Ideally, home is a safe environment with boundaries, supervision, and openness, but there is always some dynamic of dysfunction in every family. In an alcoholic parent situation, children learn quickly not to have friends over because their residence is a completely unpredictable environment. Since it is so turbulent, there's no such thing as planning ahead, and there may be little supervision or connection. These children don't feel loved or wanted. In many cases, they are forced to become the parent; cooking, cleaning, shopping and caring for younger children, and even their own parents. It's confusing and frightening.

Your first relationship is with your parents, and it sets the stage for every relationship you will have afterwards. If this is familiar, you are probably already aware that you will repeat this behavior as an adult if you don't reset your expectations. Some children work hard to change their parents instead of working toward changing their own patterns. Repatterning requires insight into your original blueprint to change it. Avoiding attachment or depending on others to meet your emotional needs is not a viable choice if you want to live an authentic life.

To feel safe and stable, you need to find a healthy connection with yourself before you can trust others. Look back at your relationships. The first step in changing your behavior is acknowledging destructive and repetitive choices. You can't repair what you don't recognize. Honest communication is a way of using your strengths and admitting your weaknesses. Talk to your partner and listen to what they tell you. Be open. It may further you to work with a therapist if you are stuck. Choose friends who have healthy relationships with each other. You can learn a lot by observation.

You Can't Change What You Don't Acknowledge/I'm Not Stubborn, I'm Just Right

Your body is your connection to your experiences. In order to bring attention to your true thoughts at this moment, you need to consciously be here. Awareness is the key to change. Our minds flip back and forth between the past, present, and future. We are always dancing on a thin tightrope of what is real and what is in our imagination. Being open to change attracts it to come in without fear. Observing nonjudgmentally needs you to embrace a practice of listening to yourself. To notice what is going on inside and outside of your body, challenge yourself to be more aware of everything you see and feel, including sounds and emotions. As time passes, consider if your mind is wandering and reel it back. What sensations surround you? Are you missing the chance to savor an experience? Reset your inner GPS to wherever you are right now, and breathe.

Training your awareness is the key to personal power. If you are fully conscious and cognizant, you have the focused ability to decide everything you do and say. What you think and choose to feel becomes second nature. Living your authentic life means paying attention to everything in your world and owning each part of yourself. It's a relief to be accepting of your whole self. It gives you the freedom to love yourself and others.

We are all creatures of habit and used to doing things a certain way, i.e., our way. Thinking outside of the box doesn't come easily to everyone. But sometimes, perceived stubbornness is not an inability to change. It can be very uncomfortable to do things differently, and the fear of failure is a good reason to keep doing things the way we always have. If it ain't broke, why fix it? Taking a risk when things are fine as they are is a chance when you've established a certain level of comfort, but there might be a different or better way to reinvent the wheel. Unless you are open to the possibility, you're the one with the attitude.

If you know someone who is argumentative, it may help alleviate frustrations if you approach them with the willingness to understand their perspective. You can assess the situation calmly by starting a conversation about the ideas or changes that need to be addressed without being confrontational. Listening to someone who remains steadfast in their inability to consider another point of view can help dissipate their anger. By allowing them to speak their piece without having to defend their position, you've opened the door to a shared resolution. It's important to understand in order to be understood. Most of us just appreciate being heard. This small kindness is an easy way to honor and respect another person as well as yourself for having the wisdom to accept that you don't know everything.

The Only Thing We Have To Fear Is Fear Itself/Freezing In The Dark Shadow Of Love

Fear is primitive. It is a powerful human emotion that warns us of threats or danger, whether perceived or real. This jeopardy presents itself in many ways within the human body, from physical to psychological. How we react is a combination of stimuli and very personal to each of us. Our brains have to quickly decide whether to confront a threat or run from it. It's an automatic response known as fight or flight. For some people, this is enjoyable. For others, a terrible experience.

Maybe you are an adrenaline seeker who loves to put yourself in thrilling situations. Extreme sports or giant roller coasters are your idea of a great recreational adventure. Those of us who prefer our excitement in a way that doesn't cause sweating palms and racing hearts have a negative response to that sort of thing. Each to his own. To combat an involuntary negative reaction, some people respond well to therapies such as hypnotism. It has been used for centuries to control many behaviors with great success. I tried it myself and found it to be useful for relaxation, as is meditation.

I have also heard of a successful kind of treatment for phobias involving snakes or airplanes. Apparently, there are treatments to help minimize alarm at the very thought of these situations, although they do sound a bit diabolical. Considering it employs repeated exposure that leads to familiarity, it sounds like a *Fear Factor* challenge and not a pleasurable one! But if you have fear that is somewhat unreasonable and not within the range of a normal response in a situation, it may need to be addressed differently. You may have the kind of anxiety that could move into uncontrollable fear that you would rather avoid.

There are so many different ways to deal with these triggers. Consult a physician and determine whether your reactions are psychological or physical in order to properly address them and reduce your discomfort. You can learn to live with your fears and get past the overwhelming panic with proper treatment. Sadly, that is not the case every time you get pierced by Cupid's arrow. You don't always get a choice when you fall in love. Sometimes, it just happens. Being so open is an incredibly vulnerable position for a human. Love can completely envelop or destroy, depending upon unpredictable circumstances, i.e., the other person's feelings.

When you open your heart to someone, the best-case scenario is that it's a reciprocal situation. The minute you reveal your innermost secret, everything changes. Unless you're sure it's mutual before you confess undying love for another, it's also a huge risk. Are you prepared for the possibility that your beloved could banish you to Dante's Second Circle of Hell (aka the dreaded Friend Zone) if they don't feel the same way, forever shattering your hopes, dreams, and quite conceivably, your existing relationship? Consider the massive risk. A perfectly lovely friendship could be destroyed with a few words. If it's not mutual, it's hard to remain friends with someone after this sort of confession.

Your monkey mind is busy envisioning all sorts of storylines that may or may not be true, so no matter what, you're going to feel pretty awful. Rejection is the kind of torture that feeds on itself. Who, what, where, how, and why will take on new proportions as your brain spins, imagining all the consequences of your impulsive action. Stop beating yourself up. So, you took a chance. Bravo for having the courage! Real love is not one sided. It takes a giant commitment and responsibility for two people to choose to accept and love each other. You have the strength to know that there is a person for you, someone who will love and cherish you back. Now have patience. Your broken heart will mend. Spring will come, birds will sing, and you will love again. Cue the strolling musicians!

We Need To Take Care of Ourselves Before We Can Take Care Of Others/Time-Out

The whole world is watching itself right now. Everyone is thinking about what they've left behind in order to move forward. Maybe this is the reset we didn't know we needed, the opportunity to discover a new way of life that's more rewarding to ourselves and each other. Could some of the things that you do need an overhaul? You have the time to examine the past and the present to consider the future. Do a 21-day meditation, start to write a journal, think about a friend who could use a call. We are all superheroes. We connect with people in different ways depending on our needs and theirs. That's how humans form bonds with other humans.

When does practicing self-care cross the line? Read my moisturized lips: it doesn't. Being aware that you need attention for your own well-being is essential. Taking time for yourself is a lovely way to honor mind and body without feeling selfish or guilty. You're not a social pariah if you decide to do a face mask and watch a movie at home instead of going out. You're merely listening to your needs. Sensible. Sometimes alone time to recharge your emotional and physical health is the best choice you can make to maintain your zen. No apology necessary.

It brings pressure down and serenity back to admit you require a moment or two for yourself. When you're feeling good inside and out, you're able to be present for the other people in your life who need attention with their own struggles. Everyone can use some compassion, so a bit of extra care goes a long way to help heal daily trauma.

You are prepared to give or receive kindness when you are well and mindful, open to both asking for it and giving it. It's a good balance and satisfying for all parties to know they are supported with love and attention. Sleep or rest both help to recover and restore your health when you're feeling stressed or tired. Take some time to read a book or binge watch a show in bed. Napping is a peaceful escape to relax body and mind away from difficult or stressful thoughts.

If you still find it difficult to practice, reach out to someone who is not in your inner circle, like a therapist or counselor. Guilt is an emotional experience that has no logical place in the application of care of yourself. Letting go of built up resentment and anger that drains you is very cathartic. Being alone to consider and process situations that are out of balance is an excellent way to evaluate personal or work relationships. Most importantly, don't give up. You can achieve harmony within by taking time to treat yourself with the patience you deserve to feel whole. It's not selfish to put yourself first. It's what keeps you present, balanced, and grateful.

Dear Fair Weather Friend/The Mind May Forget, But The Body Will Remember

You know who you are. You're the friend who is always late, when you don't cancel our date, after waiting until the last minute to confirm -in case you get a better offer. Whew!

So, we are done.

I have given you many chances to be my friend. Look at the bright side: You have an opening for someone else who is willing to let you dump your garbage on them. There is no room in your schedule for an authentic relationship with me. And that's the first requirement on my amended friendship application. Revelation! Show me your friends and I will tell you who you are. But before I bid you adieu, let me leave you with some parting advice that I assume you will ignore. I'm going to say it anyway. Being a hummingbird flitting from flower to flower keeps you from getting to know yourself.

Recognize that your life could be so much fuller. It's going to take some reflection and hard work, but it's a lot more rewarding than being on a fruitless search for elusive happiness. You aren't going to find it. Stop. Take a breath. I'll tell you a secret. Everything you need is already inside your toolbox. You have to decide that the person you are is essential and valuable. No one can tell you who you are when you know who you are. The universe has sent you a custom-made outfit that fits perfectly. Why would you want to wear anything else?

Childhood trauma triggers emotional and physical reactions that stand in the way of healthy adult relationships. Physical or emotional abuse, sexual assault, and neglect cause terror and anxiety. People who have experienced traumatic events risk developing PTSD, a psychological condition. When children live through abuse, it affects their developing brains and limits the capacity to trust others. They often create a false self to get through daily life, craving any attention so much that they are willing to accept a relationship, even a bad one that appears perfect on the outside. Their unspeakable hurt and shame are buried under the cheerful demeanor they display to the world. Behind closed doors, life is very different.

Those in denial may not realize how deeply their old trauma is affecting them. Psychological damage can cause serious and lifelong pain to the body. It is difficult to recover from debilitating stress without help. A healthy relationship takes introspection and the willingness to get the necessary aid to move forward. Without repatterning their original blueprint, they will never learn to embrace the beauty of their authentic selves. Everyone deserves love. It is crucial for well-being to move beyond the pain of the past to heal. Bodies store memories that can be reframed positively with a trained professional counselor.

Life is what happens when you're busy making other plans.

—John Lennon

Is Different Wrong?/Approve

I am surprised at how overwhelmed and stressed people are now, especially those who've barely begun to live. Even with support, living your best life is a journey of occasionally treacherous moments. If you learn to use your toolbox, the instincts you were born with will guide you forward in the most organically beautiful way. Self-examination is absolutely necessary if you want to achieve inner happiness. Humans need connection. Put down the phone, turn off the computer, and have a conversation with each other. Don't know how to start? Try "*How was your day*?" and actually listen to the answer.

I once took an improvisation class. Since it was unscripted, I had to listen to the other actors' words to react and then respond to whatever they said. It reminded me that it's quite nice to have a spontaneous, even nonsensical exchange with another person. You might learn something, teach something, or laugh at something. Whenever people share thoughts or opinions, it's a win. Knowledge is powerful.

When I look at the life I was born into, I see choices I made because of my circumstances. Before I knew how to use my toolbox, my world was limited to those experiences and expectations. Once I committed to know and accept myself, better choices became available to me. Because I was able to "*own*" all my parts, including some that I didn't particularly like, I now understand the need for every piece of me. I make decisions based on all options, not just the ones that others presented me with.

If you accept yourself, no one can tell you who you are because you already know. The parts of you that you use daily and the parts that you bring out when necessary hold equal status. Love yourself first and you have started the process of connection to yourself and others. Our differences reflect our sameness. It's much easier not to judge others when you are comfortable with yourself. Throw away the pressure of disappointing others by giving yourself the gift of self-acceptance. Loving yourself opens your heart to infinite possibilities.

I wonder if the word approval is a negative word, or just a negative word if you let it define you in other people's eyes. Remember how good you felt when you praised a friend's accomplishment. Everyone loves to be seen positively. It's not an approval. It's an acknowledgement of achievement. Approval can be a good thing when it's given without strings or expectations.

Be aware of all sides of yourself. Consider the experience of a negative interaction by examining your choices and assessing them honestly. Think about why it made you feel bad. Was your behavior one that you could reevaluate? Hurt can be diffused by acknowledging and accepting why an action caused pain. Another person's disapproval might have nothing to do with you. The criticism could have been an unconscious projection toward you of something they don't like about themselves. It is essential for your inner compass to lead the way. Mine navigated childhood through a jungle of people who lied and abused me. As an adult, I acknowledge no longer needing the protection of absolutes. I am able to choose my own path. We all have the ability for growth. We are only stuck until we choose to move forward.

Ordinary People/Honor

Being extraordinary is a goal our society greatly values. We heap shame upon ourselves and others in the pursuit of perceived excellence. We demand constant and committed achievement, often forgetting to enjoy the simple purity of living. Why is there shame in being ordinary? We waste hours trying to please other people whom we may or may not disappoint, depending on whether we have lived up to their idea of what is valuable. We so want to fit in that we conceal the parts of us that would be perceived unworthy. We devalue ourselves to a common currency in order to barter our way into the herd. It is so important to us that we even shame ourselves. It's an emotion that we bow to regularly to feel socially accepted.

I offer an alternative for you to consider. Just choose a different crowd. Spoiler alert: there is an entire tribe of people who match your needs out there. When you believe in who you are, you're able to assess what you need, want, and desire. The only way to survive shame is to develop a healthy relationship with yourself. Shame doesn't like empathy, especially for oneself. If you are silent or secretive, or sit in judgement, you foster it, both in and around you. Having the courage to be ordinary means embracing your vulnerability. To be present in any relationship requires you to start with yourself. Be honest. Let go of shaming yourself because you don't fit the mold. Being different is gift. Wouldn't life be boring if we were a world of cookie-cutter people? Love your extraordinary ordinariness and be yourself. Besides, everyone else is already taken.

Your tribe is formed from a system of shared beliefs. The energy you send out into the world attracts others to you. If your personal code is honorable, you radiate a bond of loyalty and trust with words and deeds that will gather like-minded people to you in strong tribal alignment. It is both healing and supportive. When you honor yourself, you are able to define your choices with conviction. By upholding important ethical standards like respect and morality, you can trust yourself and the members of your tribe to honor promises and commitments to others. The strength and positivity of the tribe are reflected in their actions and provide stability to the entire group.

Honoring promotes love and compassion. It is nearly impossible to move forward without encouragement and pride from yourself and the people who surround you. These choices are significant in creating a benevolent system that includes empathy and kindness for everyone. Your health is affected by the energy you hold inside your body. Daily happiness and gratefulness are impacted by the ability to authentically know yourself. Feel confident in your choices, stand up for yourself, and own your right to be the person you are. You deserve respect.

You are imperfect, permanently and inevitably flawed.
And you are beautiful.

—Amy Bloom

Is It Cold In Here Or Just Me?/How Do You Find Empathy For The Loss Of Your Childhood?

Detachment seems like a disconnect. It can feel like you're walking away from others when in fact you are walking toward owning yourself. Only you can determine your life's path. Every relationship and experience you have—past or current—invite you to re-examine and evaluate your choices and feelings. Listening to yourself drowns out the voice of the outside world, allowing your mind to organize and create a personal plan of forward movement.

When you dismiss the invisible boundaries that hold you captive in an uncomfortable situation, you become liberated. Letting go of the perception that you are limited by anyone else's projections frees you to evaluate what your goals are and puts you on the path to achieve them. Trust your inner voice to answer the questions you've asked other people. They don't know you like you know yourself.

How do you find empathy for the loss of your childhood? Go back to it. If your parents are still alive, ask them to own their mistakes. It's possible they have evolved since the time you were a child and are now able and willing to apologize to you. This is a giant cathartic move forward for everyone. It is as healing for them to admit their past behavior as it is for you to hear. But be prepared. You may encounter an entirely different scenario. What if they get angry or defensive instead and make excuses for their poor parenting? As an adult, accept that you can't change their version of your childhood. Let it go. You don't need them to validate you.

Replace a negative blueprint with a loving one. Stop blaming yourself for the past errors you made or the feelings you have. Your parents' choices gave you the perspective necessary to honestly appraise your own actions. Begin to repair the damage you suffered by freeing yourself of any old judgements that do not serve you. Decide what you are willing to accept or reject.

No matter what some people believe, there is no such thing as a perfect childhood. Take responsibility to willingly parent yourself. View your wounds as positive lessons toward the personal growth essential for separation and evolution. The best and most authentic book of instructions on how to parent is the one written by your own experiences. We learn by sorting 147 our past; embracing or rejecting with compassion and forgiveness. Accept that nothing is completely good or bad. There is an opportunity in every moment when you choose to be grateful for all of them.

Invitation Only/Empowering And Shifting Old Perceptions To Move Forward

When I was 16, a teacher gave me the best advice I've ever received. She said that only I knew who I was and to never let anyone else define me. A valuable lesson, even though it took me ten years to understand and embrace it. No one can hurt you if you don't let them in. Make sure they're on your guest list. It's very likely that your strengths threaten them in some way.

You don't need to compare yourself to others. They have strengths that may be different from yours. They just don't know it yet. You choose yourself first and then you find your tribe. Or they may find you first, since there's a constant search party out looking for individuals who find comfort in their own skins. My son wanted so badly to be on the baseball team when he was young. It was pretty evident that he was never going to shine at this sport. Unfortunately, it was middle school, the unfiltered jungle of teenage angst. When his teammates told him, "You suck," he came home crying and disheartened. We talked about it and I suggested he quit the team (I don't like quitting but watching his despair was awful). He gave it some thought and decided that being on the team was fun even if he warmed the bench more often than he ever held a bat. For three years, he stayed on the team and had a great bonding experience with the other guys anyway. Happiness was his, observing the butterflies in the far field.

In order to move forward from your past, you need to face it and take accountability for what has happened along the way. This acceptance will help you learn from all of your experiences and allow you to break any stuck and negative cycles. You can then make clear decisions about exactly what you want to invite into your life. The blueprint you have created along the way may no longer serve you now. It's time for your old interpretations to be revisited. Where you were once powerless, you are now in control of your choices and opportunity. Use the past as a tool to create your future. The power you feel when you let go of stagnant and hurtful memories is life changing. No longer do you need to hide or blame yourself and others for what has happened to bring you to this point.

The pain and sadness you held on to then helps you to understand the empathy you now embrace and shifts your negativity into positivity. You are free of judgements when you look differently at the reasons you stored these moments in your life. The anger and resentment are replaced by gratitude for the lessons life gave you. Moving yourself forward by making a conscious decision to accept and release those feelings affects negativity and strips any words of their power. It's a gift to discover and love yourself. I remember my stepmother telling me many times that she never worried about me. As a child, I assumed it was because she didn't care. After all, she had a daughter the same age as me and her attention was there. As an adult, I see that it was because I was independent and could be trusted to handle situations when her attention was needed elsewhere.

I see how being strong has served me well in my life.

I feel good about what made me once feel bad.

Look for your own memories and replace them with your new interpretations.

*Success is most often achieved by those who don't know
that failure is inevitable.*

—Coco Chanel

Set The GPS . . . To Your Happy Place!/Try Not To Laugh

Normal anxiety is when you feel a bit stressed taking a test or sitting through a job interview. It might actually motivate you to focus better and be mindful, but if your anxiety is so severe that you experience paralyzing symptoms like heart palpitations, excessive sweating, and threatening thoughts without warning, you are suffering from an anxiety disorder.

This disabling condition can cause even more consternation because it limits your ability to function in the world. If you want to regain control of your life, be diligent and seek proper treatment to help cope with the severe panic you experience.

If the anxiety is mild, try connecting with friends or family. Join a support group, you'll soon see that you are not alone. Go out with people and talk about what causes you to feel worried, or choose a memory of person or place that pulls you out of the rabbit hole. Whenever I start to feel panicky, I focus on my grandmother's face. It reminds me how she fearlessly confronted difficulties and allows my unnecessary fears to quickly subside. I am almost instantly calmed. Relaxation techniques like meditation or breathing are useful exercises too. Aerobics, dance, walking, or swimming are fun and move your mind away from repeating or distressing thoughts.

Find a strategy that works for you. If these suggestions don't help, consider visiting your doctor for medical or behavioral therapy. The specific benefit of any option is personal and needs thorough consideration and discussion before choosing the best one for you. Anxiety disorders respond well to appropriate treatments and can be managed. Be proactive. Break free from overwhelming worry. Studies have shown that adults laugh at least 20 times a day, and children up to 200. You can laugh as a response to someone else's laughter or when you're excited or happy. A thought or dream can bring on a smile that turns into a laugh.

Laughter has survived evolution. Animals laugh when they are tickled or playing. Check out National Geographic. Apes and chimpanzees adore a good giggle. Doesn't it make you laugh just watching Internet videos of them cavorting with each other? There are theories that even rats do it (although maybe a bit less since their food sources are blocked by all the COVID-19 restaurant closures). Laughter is awesome, even if no one else is laughing. I laugh at myself all the time. What! I'm funny! If you laugh at yourself, it disperses whatever judgement you or anyone else could put on you. Almost every situation has the potential to be funny. However, laughing at the expense of others is never nice and can be hurtful. Think about what's appropriate before you say it. Consider whether you would like someone to say it to you.

Laughter helps us bond. It's not a cultural thing, nor a learned behavior. We are born with the involuntary ability to laugh. In other words, you just can't help it. People laugh for all sorts of reasons, including excitement or nervousness. Sometimes a giggle can turn into uncontrollable laughter, so much that your sides hurt. A positive frame of mind makes you feel better for sure. Laughter stimulates your heart, lungs, and muscles and releases endorphins. If you are stressed, it can help invigorate your circulation, decrease blood pressure, relieve tension and pain. Choose to spend your time with people who make you laugh. These are the same people who will laugh at your jokes and stories. It's really gratifying and relaxing to feel accepted and comfortable. Coping with the world is stressful. Connecting with others positively is essential to happiness.

The best and most beautiful things in the world cannot be seen or even touched - they must be felt with the heart.

—Helen Keller

Time To Change/Hope

Linear time is a constant series of events that lead toward something, including human survival. This timeline records the history of our growth and progress and provides stories of our successes. Because it is not absolute, it simultaneously bestows infinite possibilities for hope while wielding the power to destroy anything it creates. It is impossible to ignore our vulnerability to its existence. If we want to transform our world, we need to hold on to the strong belief that we can make a difference by working together.

Time is linked to change and change to awareness. Linear time invites progress when we employ negotiation and attention to continue to move forward. Humanity must have reverence and reference for what came before. Our capacity to undertake a conscious continuum for the evolutionary process remains to be seen. To do so, we must first accept the importance of repatterning our collective blueprint. The past is a guidebook to the present and our future.

We are living in complex times. As we age, time moves evermore quickly. Every moment that we are alive is important and lovely. We can choose to measure life with a clock, but why? Life is so much richer and delightful when we use time to experience appreciation and compassion for ourselves and each other. We have been handed a clear message by this pandemic.

Time is more than the measure of minutes and hours on a clock. It is about connections to ourselves and each other. If we need to adjust our linear limits to enjoy the wonders and delights of every single moment, let's use our time to do it. The whole world is at sixes and sevens right now. Hope is not easy to hold on to when everything around us is constantly changing and uncertain. How can we manifest positivity with this unexpected paradigm shift? There is a logical way out of the present darkness. We must not allow fear to stop us from moving forward.

Our world is filled with brave and generous people whose unbroken spirit has united to demonstrate empathy and compassion for others. From the essential workers who pick up our garbage and run our buildings to the doctors and nurses who staff our hospitals, the farmers and grocers who feed us, and the volunteers who care for our sick and elderly, we are a strong force.

The change is exciting. Call on your inner leader to spread the message that we will find our strength in each other. The pandemic is a reminder that we need to come together to reset our world. It's time to join in solidarity to rebuild our relationships and our country. United we stand. Divided we fall.

Whoever is happy will make others happy too.

—**Anne Frank**

How Do You Find Yourself When You Don't Know Who You're Looking For?/Healing The Wounded Child

I've been thinking about this conundrum a lot lately. It's not always comfortable to examine the things we unconsciously do. Like breathing, we have been conditioned both from birth and experiences - pleasant and unpleasant - to make choices. Your true self, already inside you from the moment you are born, is yearning for freedom from the restrictions you've placed on it. Nature and nurture share our daily development. We need to take a deep breath in and learn how to release it out into the world as positive energy.

Never underestimate the power of yourself. The best thing about becoming a leader is that you can pick your own tribe. Look at the decisions that were made for you as a child. Now examine the choices you have made in your friendships—the people you hold the closest. It's possible that without even realizing it, you've mirrored the relationships you saw between your parents and others in your life. No matter what sort of home you grew up in, your choices were affected by that environment, whether you're conscious of it or not. You could experience poor self-esteem from exposure to a blueprint that includes abandonment, addiction, negligence, fear, detachment, or other physical/mental abuse. Just as easily, you may feel inadequate for other reasons that have nothing to do with you.

But at this moment, you hold all the power. Whatever your past was, it brought you here because you want a positive change. You have the ability right now to move forward with the people you personally choose. This is a magnificent opportunity to invite like-minded people into your life. You can examine, embrace, or reject everything you were exposed to as a child. The old patterns you've been following no longer own you if you let them go. You deserve love and affection. When you are ready to accept and love yourself, you'll attract it back from others. It's a self-fulfilling prophecy that will change your life.

Unseen Scars/Puzzle Pieces

What doesn't kill you makes you stronger, right? Not exactly. How you handle the trauma is what makes you stronger. Going through a terrible experience will certainly change you, but surviving the pain of the horror depends entirely on the work you put in afterward. Enduring residual trauma makes you question everything about the world you live in. How could this happen? *Why did it happen to me?* You are suddenly forced to examine your fears and perceived responsibility, dissecting every belief you thought would keep you safe. Meanwhile, multiplying repercussions of the original upheaval cause further chaos and dysfunction. You replay the event in a futile effort to understand the guilt and shame you feel. Your ability to recover is compromised.

You don't deserve what happened to you. No one deserves trauma. However badly you're wounded, using the agony to hurt yourself or anyone else is destructive and continues a downward cycle. A disturbing event causes disruption but also brings the opportunity for personal growth if you are open to it. What actually matters in your life? This is your chance to look at what's important to you to assist in an appreciation of your own fragile mortality. Maybe the things you have been taking for granted are more important than you once realized, and this is the time to repattern the way you communicate that message to yourself and the people around you. If you look at the trauma as a reason for change, you create the distance necessary to gain wisdom and the resilience to release anger, rebuilding your self-esteem.

Moving on from trauma is only possible if you learn from it. It empowers you greatly to share your narrative to a supportive network of friends, family, or therapist. Your healing depends on your desire to talk about the pain. When the story is outside of you, it can no longer infiltrate you. How easy is it to end a relationship, a job, or a complete change in your world? People tout the importance of closure to alleviate managing adjustment to a life-shaking loss of something or someone. When you experience profound grief, it derails your comfort and can even challenge your very identity. You may lose faith in God or humanity and begin to question everything that put you on this unkind path to hopelessness and sadness.

Loss is truly a significant disruption for humans. It is the deepest, darkest, lowest form of disappointment, a virtual or literal death caused by an unwelcome event. To recover at all, you must find a way to rise anew out of the ashes of your feelings. Accept the pain by allowing the possibility that you may not get the answers you want. Complete resolution is seldom possible. No matter how carefully you put together the puzzle of what happened, all the pieces may not be there, leaving you to question why and how any of this happened.

Take responsibility for your actions, even if you don't understand the way others think or behave. Go slowly, using the time you need to settle into the reality that life is not always benevolent. I find writing about things that confuse or upset me helps in the process of healing. While I personally don't believe it's possible to achieve absolute closure, I do believe the past can teach you lessons today to accept what you cannot change. Every day is a blank page in your book that you can fill with your choices.

You Didn't Need To Hear That/ There Is A Way To Speak Your Mind

Do you feel shame when other people's opinions don't agree with yours? Whatever your friends or family members say or do doesn't represent you unless you agree with it. You have absolutely no control over anyone else's actions, and it is entirely your privilege as a free-thinking individual to choose the way you react to judgements. It does feel like pressure when someone you are close to and don't want to upset is not respectful of your feelings.

Take a moment to think about what they have said or done. It's up to you to make up your own mind about how you feel and respond. Some people think if they talk loudly or bully you, they will sway your opinion. That might even be their sole motivation. Maybe they're jealous of you about something else, and this passive-aggressive attack is the way they bypass their own insecurities. They may lash out at you and be completely unaware that their misplaced anger is actually about themselves. Don't take it personally. We're all trying to do our best to move forward. It's just a lot harder if you don't know who you are. Spend time getting to know all of your strengths. Welcome your strongest self to applaud your unabashed right to be an inspirational individual.

There is a way to speak your mind and be heard without creating negativity. Thinking about how to frame your thoughts before saying them out loud makes you more aware of how your opinions sound to others. When you listen to the words in your head first, it becomes easier for you to say what is important in a way that will make others more open to listening to you. People are willing to pay attention to what you have to say, even criticism, if you recognize the needs and feelings of others. Sometimes unfiltered words fly out of your mouth before you pause to consider the effect they may have once they are spoken.

It happens to everyone. You may be in a heated argument or feel that you're not being heard or considered. When you are in that situation, try to remember to take a deep breath and a few moments to hear yourself before you speak. One small word can feel like an arrow to someone you care for when it's hurled in anger. It may wound them for a long time afterward. Apologizing is a perfectly acceptable way to acknowledge and dissipate any hurt you may have caused to another person. "I'm sorry" is a very powerful statement. Anger is an emotion we all feel. How we deal with that is what makes us use it positively. Without emotions we would not be able to express joy as well as sadness or any of the other things that make us human.

Is Good Enough The New Perfect?/
Be Well

The perceived importance of being viewed as perfect is overrated. It makes me wonder if this is a reason why some people are having such a hard time with quarantine boredom. In these very difficult and unprecedented times, it is easy to lose hopefulness. We have to remind ourselves and each other that being messy is a real part of being human. Occasionally, all of us make a poor choice or an unfortunate decision. The takeaway is in how we handle a situation that goes sideways, and if we rebound. Being solution-oriented and finding resolution is a much better option than heaping blame or shame on an imperfect moment.

Learning to enjoy your own time can be a positive experience. There are many hours in a day. You could read a book on a subject that intrigues you, watch an old film, paint a watercolor 166 masterpiece, cook an impressive chef's meal, write a great novel, call your mom or dad and tell them how much you appreciate them, take an online class and knit a blanket, make a social distancing dinner date with four dear friends, paint a room bright yellow, or if you're feeling ambitious, build a treehouse in the backyard. Think of an activity you've always dreamed about trying but never had time to do . . . and do it!

Look inside your inner toolbox. Everything you need is right there waiting for you. You don't have to be perfect. It's a lot more satisfying to be good enough and messy than miserable and deflated because you can't achieve perfection. Connection is the beginning of beginning.

We are born with the innate need to look for it outside of ourselves, but the most powerful connection we can make is the one between our own mind and body. This link is primal and essential to well-being.

The way we feel, the emotions we display, and the choices we make directly correlate to the balance between mind and body. Our outward moods are an indicator of inner mental and physical stability. A positive attitude in thought and behavior is integral for total wholeness. 167 The messages sent between the brain and the rest of the body affect blood pressure, heart rate, sleep patterns and appetite.

The scientific discovery of a connection between mind and body is relatively new. Thirty years ago, a study of group mindfulness therapy by David Spiegel, Director of Psychosocial Research at Stanford University, revealed that women with breast cancer who participated had less pain and an improved quality of life compared to women who received traditional care alone. His findings have been tested numerous times since, establishing a proven connection between mind and body. In short, your brain has a direct influence on the way your body heals.

Taking care of your mental health greatly affects the quality of your life. Well-being is directly improved by the choices you make to achieve connection and equilibrium. The body has an important impact on the mind's maintenance. Get in touch with yourself and understand that food choices, a regular exercise routine, and stress management all contribute to a lifestyle of genuine good health.

Who Are You Going Believe—Me Or Your Lying Eyes?/Is Jealousy Actually Good For You?

Of course, we have all lied about something. It can occasionally be hard to look at the truth without wincing. You don't have to be a good liar to convince yourself and others of anything if you are willing to overlook a fact or two. It just depends on whether you care to know who you really are or prefer to be who you say you are. The Internet has made it even easier to be anyone you want to be. Just put an airbrushed-to-the-max picture of yourself on Instagram or TikTok. Are you the clever catfish who hand selects a stranger's photo from the bevy of beauties on Facebook? All it takes is a click for instant transformation. Who's going to check you, boo? Um . . . reality?

Let's get down to the lowest common denominator: Who and why are you hiding? What is the reason you don't want others to know the real you? Maybe you don't like the real you because you don't know the real you. But . . . if *you* don't accept the real you, how can anyone else ever truly know you? There's a reason why you are who you are. You may not like everything about yourself. Examine the choices you've made and the ones you still make. It's time to let go of what no longer serves you. It's not hard to move forward when you make the commitment to get to know yourself without judgement. No one judges you as harshly as you judge yourself. It's a waste of your precious time to hold on to negativity.

Acknowledging trauma is a big step toward freeing yourself from the past. Make amends to people you've hurt. Forgive yourself for any decisions you've made that have kept you stuck and release yourself from shame, guilt, and pain. A good therapist will help you uncover your true self. It's a necessary journey if you want to plug the holes in your daily life and relationships. Choose today to move forward. It might not be as bad as you thought. Take a moment to notice where it came from. Jealousy is a wake-up call. It can offer insight to help you identify what you value. It may inspire you to try a new experience. If it is about recognition, look into your inner toolbox and find the strength within to claim the appreciation you desire.

Low self-esteem or insecurity causes anxiety. Obsessive behavior is damaging to any relationship. What do you want or need? How can you achieve it? Being aware of your goals can be constructive in the pursuit of contentment when you embark on positive action to take you toward them. Why are you feeling this discomfort? Be honest with yourself. Accept that acknowledgment of jealousy is normal. Communicate with your partner, friends, or family members. Explain your feelings calmly to discuss a solution. Being direct is a constructive approach to a potentially hostile situation. Work together to achieve harmony and dispel negativity. Whether real or imagined, the threat to damage a relationship requires exploring and repairing. If the feelings are too overwhelming, consult a therapist to help with a satisfactory resolution.

The Eye Of The Beholder/"One Sees Clearly Only With The Heart. Anything Essential Is Invisible To The Eyes." ~ de Saint-Exupéry

The way our brains react to beauty is only one way of determining perception and interest. Someone whose looks you admire may not stir those same feelings in another person. Physical beauty is an enticing wrapper but completely subjective. It's all about your choices.

The photo you swipe right to is another person's quick swipe left. To me, the most interesting part of a human being is inside rather than outside. True beauty is often invisible to the eye. A physically unattractive person can be absolutely stunning if they are funny, kind, and generous. It automatically raises their appeal. The same goes for a person who has a mean-spirited, negative temperament. No, thank you; I'll pass. Life is too short to spend it around people who are closed and cruel.

Wouldn't it be wonderful if we could judge each other by our hearts? Hearts can tell us so much more about who we are because they have experienced both love and pain. Full of passion and wonder, hearts are able to show compassion and forgiveness in every circumstance. There are so many different ways to give and receive love. We can love and love again. When you are in touch with yourself, your inner world is illuminated and inviting. Beauty fades, but love endures and grows in a magnificent way if we open ourselves to the experience.

Antoine de Saint-Exupéry, the author of one of my favorite books, *The Little Prince,*

so perfectly expressed the need for connection with others, especially when we are alone. Our vivid memories of the people and experiences we treasure can carry us through difficult separations from each other. It is necessary to look with our hearts in those moments when we feel sadness for whom and what we have lost. Our ability to hold hope and share connection with each other is universally essential. When our eyes are blind and cannot find what they are looking for, our hearts remain clear. Everything and everyone you love is with you, even if you can't be together right now.

The secret is this:

We are held together by each other.

Close your eyes. Whatever you need will appear if you hold in your heart.

Love is a paradox, fragile yet resilient.

You Are Not The Same Person You Were When You Were Born/ When Temptation Knocks, Do You Answer The Door?

Along the way, you have imprinted your blueprint with many choices. Some have been made for you and others by you. These decisions created your personal path, and along any path lurks both danger and opportunity. Compassionate understanding of yourself and others is the growth you need to move forward in positivity and love. In order to invite change, examine those experiences and expectations. Maybe they are no longer valid and don't serve who you are right now. You attract what you give.

Happiness and gratitude are powerful allies if you choose positivity as your guide. Every moment since you were born, your choices have brought everything into your life. When you pick the direction you want to take, you have placed an order with the universe. Your journey unfolds, twisting and turning your path according to your choices. You may not be looking for temptation, but occasionally it finds you.

Sometimes parents engage in unethical choices for their children if they feel it's the only way to achieve a fair result. To an outsider, their behavior may look skewed, but they feel quite confident that they've made a perfectly reasonable decision. My friend had this exact situation with her son. She used her sister's address to get him into a more desirable school district than the one in her town. "Why shouldn't he have the advantages he deserves," she said indignantly. "Life isn't fair." She's not alone. Plenty of parents have made similar choices to advance their children's education. Perhaps they weren't given opportunities themselves and feel they need to right the wrong they suffered. Whatever rational they choose, to them it's valid, logical, and deserved.

I know someone who cheats on his partner but goes to weekly confession with his priest to absolve the sins. He feels even better after he throws ten bucks in the collection basket. It lets him off the hook, feeling confident that the slate is wiped clean. Then there are those who believe rules don't apply to them. If a cashier forgets to ring up a bag of shrimp, they see it as the universe giving them what they deserve anyway. It's the clerk's fault for not paying attention. Or they justify it by recounting the many dollars they've spent at that store, "which by the way is ridiculously overpriced." No matter what, there's always a waiting excuse to positively frame anything you do. At least to you.

How you choose to act is an indication of who you are. Some situations challenge moral principles because they are more complex than others. When you have a clear understanding of right and wrong, your inner compass should guide you correctly. However, if you are confused, you may try to rationalize your behavior with a self-serving justification to assuage guilt and feel good about a decision. Your interpretation of an event can influence you selectively to make an amoral choice in order to get the desired outcome. When you lack concrete rules to maneuver through temptations life throws in your path, you could decide to manipulate your possibilities. Will you? Who are you?

Don't be satisfied with stories, how things have gone with others.
Unfold your own myth.

—Rumi

The Happiness Box/
Invisible Shackles

Don't we all wish for that elusive thing called happiness? The search began the very moment we opened our eyes for the first time and instinctively felt an intangible strength and will to find our je ne sais quoi, even though we didn't yet have the words to describe why we craved it.

Human beings are born seeking connection, beginning with ourselves. Babies explore their bodies, voices, and anything else they can see or touch. Every discovery is a new delight because there is no judgement. By understanding and owning each of your qualities, you let go of the judgement you've collected along the way to becoming an adult. You accept yourself and open your heart to embrace love from others.

When your mind is clear, you see the essential beauty in every one of your qualities and the qualities of others. As you collect life experiences, you invite like-minded people into your tribe. Desiring perfection holds you back from living the authentic, compassionate life you long for. Acceptance of your whole self is necessary to break down the protective walls of fear that you previously erected. You may have needed them before you recognized that there is good in every lesson, even the painful ones.

Once you begin living your authentic life, you no longer need to arm yourself. When you know who you are, defending your choices is unnecessary. It is your imperfections that make you wonderful and unique. When you form a bond of understanding and acceptance with yourself, you are on the path to making healthy decisions. If you don't have respect for yourself, it becomes very easy to let others decide who you are. The choices you make reflect your self-esteem. Do your choices enhance your spirit or drain your power?

Make a conscious decision to move forward using your inner toolbox to determine the way you judge yourself. Your energy and power are magnified and strengthened by your courage. The effect of the world outside you is affected by the lessons you learn from observations and experiences. Because fear and anxiety can sneak in so easily, remember to appreciate and believe in yourself to get past those moments.

Repattern your blueprint. Create a daily affirmation that reminds you of your own authority.

I am . . .

If you know who you are then no one can tell you who you are. Every part of you is valuable. Living your life authentically is the gift you give yourself.

‹

When You Hurt Someone's Feelings Do You Acknowledge It?/Are You Laughing At Me Or With Me?

An innocent remark can trigger a volatile reaction. Maybe you didn't realize the impact of your action when you reacted or responded negatively. Were you angry about something else? Or was it simply a misunderstanding because of the way it was expressed? How you communicate feelings is as important as the feelings themselves.

When I was a child, my father often told me that anger was my favorite emotion but never asked why I was angry. Many years later, I began to navigate the trapped feelings and words I had learned to hold inside. I now understand that my father had been projecting his own frustrations onto me. My unhappiness at not being heard was a reflection of his inability to have empathy for himself and, consequently, me. Understanding and letting go of the unresolved anger was worth the introspection. It taught me to be a parent who listens and hears my own child. I thank my father for teaching me how to embrace what he was unable to see. I encourage you to find comfort in seeking help to love your authentic self.

Unlike most of us who find laughter contagious, some people don't think it's funny at all. They feel anxious and defensive, as if others are calling them out or making fun of them. This sort of hypersensitivity reveals a deep insecurity that keeps them from building intimate relationships with other people. The fear of being laughed at is called gelotophobia. It happens early in childhood when an infant feels they can't trust their caregiver to be there when they need them. If the adult is unable or unwilling to provide this essential care, the child experiences excessive fearfulness. This leads to an insecure attachment style by continuing to inflict feelings of shame and unworthiness.

If a child grows up this way, it becomes very difficult to form and continue satisfying relationships. When a parent doesn't pay attention, the child learns not to care, choosing to become independent and stay away from close connections with others. Their approach to survival embraces the discomfort within the anxiety of the attachment. This precludes the possibility of a fulfilling experience with another person.

Conversely, an avoidantly attached gelotophobe might become overly dependent and demanding. They may feel the need to be the center of attention, especially from their mothers. As adults, they continue to exhibit the same behavior in a clingy or jealous way, sabotaging any possibility of a healthy union between a couple. They are able to experience sexual liaisons with others without true intimacy because they're not emotionally committed. It is easy for them to feel disparaged and belittled, especially from a partner. They are trapped in the senseless maze of a continuous search mode. Look carefully at the way you respond to laughter. When people are laughing, it is probably not about you. If they are, maybe you are taking yourself too seriously. Lighten up and have a laugh at your own expense. It's boring and completely ridiculous to be perfect. I'm laughing at the very idea of it.

Sliding Doors/You're Welcome . . . To Leave

Fate is what happens when you don't take responsibility for your life, while destiny is what happens when you commit to growing, learning, and taking chances. It comes through your own active and conscious decisions. Our path in life is almost never clearly marked. We don't know exactly what we can expect to find down any road.

One choice you make can affect everything that happens from that moment on. Consider all offered opportunities using your intuition to guide you. You choose your destiny when you pay attention to the signs that are constantly coming into your viewfinder. They can be easy to miss, especially if you're waiting for fate to find you.

Fate is a serendipitous and fickle thing. It can happen just because you showed up. Consequences can be amazing or brutal depending on place and time. Relying on it is ill-advised, but destiny is well within your reach if you want to live your best life.

Discovering your true self takes real introspection. Who you were born as does not have to define you.

Use your inner toolbox to move forward and repattern your old blueprint. There is no limit to where you can go when you discover how powerful and satisfyingly it is to love yourself. You have the ability to be who you were born to be and to achieve the attainable goals you choose to reach. **Fate** is that which you cannot change. **Destiny** is that which you're meant to do. Why do certain situations and people keep showing up in our lives? Because we invite them! When we don't own and accept every part of ourselves, we attract people who negatively mirror back what is inside us.

Think about something you don't like about yourself. Instead of burying it, look at why you resist this trait. The aspects you dislike in others are often the very things you subconsciously battle. Until you face them in yourself, you can't face them in others. Your ego often gets caught up in judgement and causes blame. Blame causes resentment. When this is happening, try looking at the situation differently. Instead of holding on to an incident where you feel wronged, see how it has benefited you. How did you grow from it? You are not a victim if you use experience as a learning tool.

The more attention you pay to the choices you make, the closer you come to embracing your entire being. It's okay to love everything you are. Each single part of you is worthy of recognition and acceptance. If you are whole, the people who gravitate toward you will be a mirror of your well self. When you let go of judging yourself, you start to attract people to your tribe who reflect the healthy view you model. Transformation is waiting for you with a shift in your perception. Accept that being perfectly imperfect is the best part of being human.

The purpose of our lives is to be happy.

—Dalai Lama

Raking The Coals/May I Refill Your Glass?

Many people have asked me what it was like to be alone for four months without leaving my apartment. Since I usually spend a lot of time on my own anyway, the biggest challenge was in not being able to see family and friends if I chose. Our building has a great staff who left mail and packages at my door. Groceries I ordered were delivered to me from a store in the neighborhood. I had everything I needed, except human touch. Turns out that is what I needed the most.

Humans are neither meant to be isolated or cloistered. We thrive best in groups, craving the comfort and challenges of tribe existence. We require meaningful relationships with others. Without support, we lose hope. In the recent past, our lives included daily interactions with others. These options are not available at the moment for most of us. The worry of contamination from COVID-19 is our new normal. Everyone is a potential carrier or victim, especially those of us who are further compromised by our age or health. Reports of deaths are rampant and constant. Mayhem rules the streets and the escalating fear is pervasive.

A few weeks ago, I left New York to visit my son whom I haven't seen in months. It has been very hard for us to interact in the usual way. We can't be our spontaneous selves as the silly things we took for granted are now the things we miss the most. There is so much misinformation about this disease that the more we are told, the less we know. Still, we feel a primal need to touch, to be touched, and to love. Connection to each other is the only thing that can get us through the pandemic divide. Hold on to hope and to each other, even if it's intangible at this moment. The power of social media has never been more important, and more frightening. Let's use it to move us together and not tear us apart.

Our world has a history of revolving and evolving, and the lessons we are learning will bring us closer. We can rise from our ashes anew and aligned. What does your worldview say about you? Do you see problems in solutions or solutions in problems? Do opportunities seem like pressures or pleasures? Apparently, "half empty" thinkers tend to be laid-back and serious. 48% don't think of themselves as pessimistic, believing that they are actually more optimistic. Maybe they consider themselves realists.

"Half full" thinkers are usually morning people, which means they get up with the will and agenda to begin the day positively. They are often busy with hobbies and social activities, which keep them free from worrying so much about the minutiae they can't change anyway. Having a positive attitude usually results in a better outcome. It can lead to a more fulfilling life when you are predisposed to consider that even negative things have value. The reality is that situations change, difficulties subside, and life moves forward.

You can choose your approach and the effect it will have on you with the way you respond to these events. Everything will pass whether you dwell on what would have, could have, or should have happened. Me? My thorns have roses.

You only live once, but if you do it right, once is enough.

—Mae West

Closing Pandora's Box/Despair

Before coronavirus was even a dystopian possibility, there was the frivolous fear of missing out (FOMO), which spawned the joy of missing out (JOMO). Both have recently been replaced with the fear of joining in (FOJI). I think I may be the poster child for JOMO. I've become more organized and productive in this enforced captivity. However, most people are reluctantly accepting that the new normal is a virtual experience. Life as we knew is not the same and may never be again.

Social media has become more important than ever for business and casual meetings. Constant updates appear on phones, iPads, and computers. There are endless platforms: Zoom, FaceTime, Marco Polo, all ways to get together or be updated on everything everyone everywhere is doing. If anything, we are more checked in than checked out. It's fun for a while—until it's not. The two extremes of FOMO and JOMO are not balanced. FOJI is a result of not knowing what is the right thing to say or do. Every day, more people get called out for things they did or said long ago. Whether their actions were hurtful then or under the bright spotlight of today's microscope, is it really fair to dissect and shame each other?

The world has imploded. If we are to effectively be held accountable and make necessary amends to those we have wronged, we'll need a new way to talk and listen to each other. I would not like to be judged by my youthful choices. I truly hope I didn't offend someone at some time, but I think it's more probable than improbable that I did. Please accept my belated but sincere apology. I'm sorry. I wouldn't have made that choice today.

The only way to move forward is to learn from the mistakes we made before we knew better. It's important to acknowledge that this time in history gives us both the opportunity to own our mistakes and the responsibility to teach our children to see others as they would like to be seen. We are all born with the ability to be loving, kind, and free of judgements. Hatred is a learned and destructive response to fear. Let's change the old paradigm to shift the world to a utopian acceptance of each other.

"All the goodness and the heroisms will rise up again, then be cut down again and rise up. It isn't that the evil thing wins — it never will — but that it doesn't die." John Steinbeck wrote this to his friend during WWII. At this moment, we are again in the path of a historical event that has repeated itself over and over. The present may look different to us because we see it through the blindered lens of now, but if we don't learn from the past, we will continue to repeat it.

The same cultural events that have precipitated our current maelstrom are familiar in world history. As our ineffective hopes are swept into a swirling pool of fear and anger at the injustices, our humanity has become skewed. We have forgotten our ability, and possibly desire, to communicate and care beyond an Instagram post or indignant tirade. We need to change this. We need to educate ourselves and move forward as one race. The human race. The only race. We need to listen. We need to speak up. We have powerful voices that need to be used. That need to be heard. Let's not let despair crush our valuable world. We are too valuable. Let's invite humanity and justice to join us to fill the chasm between us with love, acceptance, and respect for each other.

It is better to fail in originality than to succeed in imitation.

—Herman Melville

Being Alone With Yourself/Am I Depressed, Or Just Lonely?

Can you ever turn off the voices in your head? The ones that can't wait to warn you about real or perceived dangers, question your decisions about everything you do or ever did, remind you that you're not good enough, smart enough, attractive enough, (and my personal favorite) do you really think you should eat that? Anything they can say to derail you and put you in your place will do. After all, who do you think you are? Worst of all, it's not what other people say. This is strictly you to you. News flash: you are your harshest critic.

But why, why would you do that to yourself? Because we all do. Solution: if you want to live a healthy life, you need to learn how to accept and love yourself. Admittedly, there are bits of you that are not 100% magnificent. An honest look inward can help you shift old patterns to accommodate a more loving approach to yourself and others. Each of us has the potential to be whomever we want to be if we are determined and committed. Summon the courage to map a plan and move forward. Choose one behavior that you'd like to change, then make a pact with yourself and follow through. Those chattering voices will eventually disappear as you replace them with more positive thoughts.

Here are a few tips to help you start thinking. Do something nice and unexpected for a friend or neighbor. Send flowers or a note telling them how much you appreciate them. You'll probably smile while you're doing this. Put clean clothes away in your drawers and dirty laundry in the hamper. Walking into a neat room will give you the boost to turn this into a daily habit. Read an autobiography of someone you admire. Figure out what it is about this person that you are drawn to. Maybe you'll learn something new about yourself. Just leave your monkey mind alone and it will leave you alone. You are perfectly imperfect, and that's the human in you.

Feeling cut off from others in a way that makes you sad? You're not alone, but you may be lonely. We all go through times that are temporarily isolating. In extreme cases, a person can experience overwhelming hopelessness or depression. Additionally, pervasive sadness can cause death in the same way that health issues like smoking and obesity affect us. This past year has been extraordinarily triggering. The stress of forced separation from friends and family, the inability to continue usual activities—or to even leave home—are tough to manage for such an extended period, especially with no fixed end date to look forward to. It's easy to feel out of control, helpless, or bored.

To combat those feelings, we need to hold our connections close. Make an effort to socialize whenever you feel the lack of human interaction. Go online to talk to a friend or make a new one on a social website. There are lots of online game forums and chat rooms. Plan your dream vacation to an exotic isle or trace your ancestral beginnings from a genealogy profile. It may be comforting to know that a cup of tea or a warm bath is a recommended physical substitute for social warmth.

The message is clear: shift your focus to include different forms of contact than the usual ways you interact with others. There are so many possibilities. Think of it this way—when was the last time you had a coffee date without getting dressed or leaving your couch?

How To Be Your Own Guru/Can You Make Things Materialize Just By Believing In Them?

If you start exploring who you are, you'll see qualities that you'd prefer to turn away from, but they are actually qualities you need to turn toward. When you accept your entire self, you heal.

Show understanding and compassion for every part of you. Be ready to nurture yourself.

Move forward toward the benevolent love that reminds you to appreciate your shadow qualities. The ones you fear might make people shun you, will instead draw people to you.

It's a simple focus. First, love yourself. Then forgive yourself for being human.

Write in your journal daily to let go of old hurts and resentments you still carry. Ask yourself why you are holding onto them. What would it take for you to release the negative beliefs that have held you back? If you're stuck in a memory that repeats in your mind, write a letter to that person or people or yourself. Say everything you need to say that you didn't at the time. Maybe you were too young to understand, scared, or both. If it was a choice, remind yourself that you have grown from that decision. You don't need to send the letter. Your forgiveness lies in the cathartic experience of writing it. Being perfectly imperfect is another way to say you love yourself.

"I discovered that my insecurities and my flaws were things that I actually need to embrace, and I let them become my superpowers."—Skylar Grey.

When you have the confidence to accept that anything can happen, you open the door to your infinite possibilities. I'm not saying that it won't work. Moving forward includes many challenges, but if you are ready to manifest your dreams, your intuition and experiences will guide you to them. You are born with all the tools you need to live a full and authentic life. Shift your focus to accept and understand that nothing you do can ever be viewed as failure. It's all a part of the marvelous journey toward becoming the person you're capable of being. You don't even need to look outside yourself. Everything you require is within you.

Nothing holds as much power as your own mind. Your insights and epiphanies are the path to true happiness when you know who you are.

When I have been the most broken is when I have made the most progress. The fears and old patterns that limited and held me back fell away with the discarded destructive behaviors that were no longer viable choices. My emotional pain turned to peace as hope, forgiveness, and the desire to embrace change pushed forward movement. The future is yours to manifest when you choose to believe in your power to turn the potential into the possible.

Reinterpreting And Letting Go/ Responsibility

Once we move forward toward love and acceptance, we begin to heal from the past. Our old blueprints are examined and sorted, allowing the person we are now to move forward. By choosing ourselves, we accept or reject what we have experienced and can design a new pattern that serves us and allows personal growth and fulfillment.

Letting go of the anger we have been holding lets in the love we have been missing. There is no need to struggle against the words and actions that caged us in the past. The beliefs we have held on to for so long have no place in the life we now choose to create for ourselves. Those beliefs had a purpose in bringing you to where you are now. Without them, you would not be here. Many came from your parents, who did their best with the tools they had been given by their parents. Without questioning or examining them, you merely accepted them—the same way they did.

Now that you're an adult, you can choose to re-examine those old core beliefs. Maybe a conscious choice or a sudden realization caused you to look at your life from a different angle. A mixed bag of memories shares the space in your mind and heart, and those memories motivate your desire for acceptance, love, and change. The world is a complicated place at the best of times. As an adult, you are able to take responsibility for your actions and gain from the lessons they provide. A lot of things transpire that you have no control over, but the events that happen to you and those you have done to yourself are solely yours.

Begin with a thoughtful understanding of your journey so far to help you navigate what is ahead of you. Having control over your choices and view of the world is key to coming to terms with yourself and moving forward. If you re-examine your past with no preemptive or defensive judgement, it will become easier to find love for every part of yourself. Your personal evolution is inevitable when you acknowledge and accept the traits in your personality that you see as "bad." Let go of the reasons you've viewed certain traits negatively. Give them extra love and compassion by embracing the belief that all your traits are positive in some way. Leave the old stories that you or others have told you behind.

You have the ability to write your own narrative.

Start with a daily affirmation of your worth. ***I am worthy of*** (_____).

Tell yourself that you own who you are and no one can tell you who you should be.

If you are not willing to risk the usual, you will have to settle for the ordinary.

—Jim Rohn

The Human Spirit Is Strong/ Sometimes You're The Windshield, Sometimes You're The Bug

Laying the foundation for a full life requires listening to your intuition and acting in a way that promotes love and compassion for yourself and others. Give up the need to know why things happen in the way they do and trust that your life is going to unfold exactly how and when it should.

Sometimes what you think you want is not what you actually need. Trying to control outcomes is counterintuitive, and life's meandering guidance is often much more fun.

The twists along your journey can be the most exciting part of your move toward the destination. You can't possibly know all of the options unless you explore some of the possibilities. When you open yourself to destiny, the world opens itself to you.

Think of a time when you had an expectation that went off course. In hindsight, you can now see how it brought you to an understanding or experience. Maybe even both. Tap into your natural ability to let intuition guide your choices. It is always there, whispering wise advice about the constant judgements and expectations that are part of human nature. Listen to it. Free will is always an option. It is not the same as strong will, which implies force. When you are honest with yourself, trusting your instincts will lead to success. Use your heart energy to empower your mental energy. This healthy combination of unified communication balances behavior and furthers the best possible result in every situation.

View change as a tunnel that leads to a shiny new adventure on the other side. Surrendering to fear is limiting. Choosing to move forward is necessary for personal progress. When an amazing opportunity I had been hoping for happened for me, I excitedly told one of my friends. Her reaction was very different than I expected. Instead of congratulating me, she said, "Why always you? Why not me?" I've often thought about that. I wonder why we can't seem to accept the reality that life isn't benevolent. Good things happen to everyone. The same applies to bad things. Everyone gets a turn at each.

If you think about your life, abundance of some kind is usually within your reach.

Why not consider why life is so good to us that we often get a lot more than we deserve? Maybe it's random, but maybe not. So, choose to being grateful for the things we get just because we exist. The daily privileges that we take for granted are a hopeful wish for many others whose struggles are whether they can feed their family or pay the rent. Think about it.

Shift a negative perception to an appreciation for the goodness that comes our way with little or no effort. If you need reminding, volunteer to serve a meal at your local soup kitchen.

The Risk Of Love Is Loss/
Shaming Sadness

I got a sad call this morning from a good friend. Her beloved Gracie, a nearly 18-year-old rescue dog, had passed away the night before. This was a huge loss for the family, but especially for my friend who had enjoyed a long and wonderful closeness with Gracie. Their coded understanding of each other was fun to witness, and many anecdotes of travels and adventures together were often part of our conversations.

Gracie wasn't well for a long time. She had a slow-growing cancerous tumor. Yet she rallied, and although there was no doubt of her inevitable death, it was still a terrible shock when it did happen. It made me wonder whether the grief we feel losing a dear pet is so different from the loss of a person we love. For some of us, our pets are family. They are cherished companions who share our daily lives and routines, teaching us responsibility and gratitude.

Animals don't judge, unlike the people in our lives. They are respectful, trustworthy, forgiving, and don't argue with us about politics or religion. We can rely on their genuine support to listen, lick away our tears, and share unconditional love, no matter what. They don't ask annoying questions we don't want to answer. We cannot always count on these qualities in our human friends, but our pets accept us as we are, flaws and all. So, it's an awful void when they die, and it hurts terribly. It's devastating.

My son cremated his hamster and put the ashes in a small box that he has reverently carried to every apartment he's lived in since middle school. The tiny urn sits right next to a Lucite enclosed signed baseball that he got from a famous player.

Choose a way that works for you to remember your pet. Some people keep framed photographs or plant a tree in the yard to honor their deceased pal.

I don't believe in closure, but I do believe that keeping memories alive in your heart can remind you in a beautiful way how lucky you were to have had that unique time with a special friend. Why do we think it's unhealthy to be sad? Because we have been conditioned to see sadness as an unproductive emotion that takes us away from the happiness and joy we should be feeling. But what if the grief is overwhelming, such as the loss of a beloved person or pet?

We are conditioned not to show our sadness on the outside, because it is negative. If you have not been taught how to check in with yourself when you feel this way, you stuff it. Some people use anger as a way to deal with their sadness. It can give a false sense of control over a situation. Others get through it with optimism. Neither of these choices works very well. You're still masking your unprocessed feelings. Maybe you sleep to avoid thinking about why you feel sad or by binge-watching TV shows, drinking, eating, or working too much. No matter how much you think you're pushing it away, it's still there.

What if you tried looking at it differently? Have you thought about listening to it? Sadness is actually really important to your well-being. It's a sign that you want to change something to grow and learn about yourself. There are positive directions that sadness can steer us.

There is no shame in expressing grief for loss because it reminds us that we are human and need connection with ourselves and each other.

If you don't allow yourself to feel every emotion, you are missing the opportunity to positively embrace and accept yourself.

Grief is a kind of love. It's an emotion that can turn many different ways. Light a candle to create an environment that makes you comfortable. Meditate. Take a walk. Write in a journal. Dance to your favorite music. Sing out loud. Talk to a good friend or a therapist. Feel into the sadness without distractions. Take the time you need to examine why you feel this way and be open to any thoughts that come up. Explore them. Asking yourself questions about your choices without second-guessing is very helpful as a way to let out any bottled up feelings.

Your memories are yours to curate. There are so many happy ones to remind you that sadness is temporary.

A Flower Blossoms For Its Own Joy/Does Your Personality Predict Your Life?

People often ask me why I write blogs. I write them because I have questions I want answers to, and sometimes writing about them helps me to reach resolution or shift my perspective. There are also times when writing gives me more questions, but that's okay too. I have a lot of curiosity about everything. I probably could have been a good forensic scientist, but that option didn't exist in the halcyon days when I was contemplating my navel. So I write.

I don't think it is a bad thing to be introspective and consider the weight of your actions. I certainly can't speculate on anyone else's choices without considering the sometimes inexplicable reasons for my own. Pen and paper have always been my inner guidance counselor, and if you've read my blogs, you already know that I began a diary in middle school and haven't stopped writing since.

I encourage you to find your inner creative muse. It helps significantly to move your thoughts into actions when you look at all the possibilities and consequences of the choices that surround you. Of course, serendipity has a preternatural ability to crash your party with the random knock of opportunity, and being in the right headspace to let it in the door can be a game changer. You cannot win if you do not play. Explore yourself. Get to know who you are to enjoy the satisfying journey to a complete and fulfilling life.

Your ability to express yourself through activities like writing, painting, baking, singing, or dancing, etc. is cathartic and soothing. Everyone has the potential to be an artist. Once you begin an honest conversation with yourself, your flower will start to bloom.

What is a predictor for a satisfying life? Who you are determines both the choices you make and the path you take. Although we all hope for a long, stable, and successful life, we need to consider specific options to achieve the best-case scenario for ourselves. Your character can be an advantage in helping you recognize your authentic self.

How much your personality influences your life is a question that is routinely explored by psychiatrists and theorists everywhere. Your attitude has been proven by studies to affect many of your outcomes. Human behavior is often influenced by social values. However, your response to situations seems to be a more determining indicator for life decisions. Are you happy? Do you feel comfortable with your economic situation? Relationships? Health? Education? What steps have you taken to ensure your total well-being? Your attitude and values steer the path of your journey and possibilities.

Examine and consider whether you can carefully shift the way you see yourself and your position to improve your life. A positive outlook can greatly guide your mental energy. Emotions also have a say in decisions. Do you let your heart rule your head or vice versa? Are you balanced in your actions and thoughts? The answer requires honesty in understanding your true motivation.

Be aware. Taking care of yourself helps you to cope effectively with whatever the world sends your way. If you're in a good place with yourself, it's easier to achieve success in your approach to planning and decision making. Your comfort and confidence wisely advise you to consult your inner toolbox for the answers necessary to move forward. Look at everything that will affect your life and consider all consequences and probabilities. While hope is essential, practicality and knowledge are useful in your quest to find your purpose. The strengths you have and way you use them shows the world who you are.

Acknowledgements

There are so many people who made this book possible. I am humbled and inspired by each of you. Thank you for believing in me. To the members of Life Essence Tribe whose love encouraged me to share my observations about the things that we all question. I am so grateful for you. To Stacy Higgins, my fellow Aquarian because without your infinite patience and artistic eye, this book would not be. You are a true friend. To Ross, for always believing in me. You have been my dearest cheerleader and supporter from the beginning. You are a truly good human. I appreciate your unconditional love and kindness. Thank you for keeping me safe and on the right path. To Annette Barrett, my oldest friend, and the reason I began this journey, thank you for opening the door. To Francesca Vuillemin, and Erika Weber, two original members of LET, thank you for your intuition and friendship along the journey. I love you both.

To Tina Tait, my sister from another mister, for always telling me the truth whether I like it or not. Your fierce instinct to protect and inspire is unparalleled. To Diane Donati, for the lucid vision to see your glass as overflowing. You remind me every day to appreciate how delightful even the smallest pleasures are. To Raquelle Dupuis, for teaching me that mind and body are intrinsically connected. You are truly gifted with patience and kindness. To Carolyn Bankston, for your ability to hear without judgement and advise with wisdom. Your support and generosity have deeply touched and changed me. To Natalie Kinghorn, for your absolute determination to own your remarkable authentic self. You inspire me every day to use my toolbox.

To Michael Melendez, for your daily smile and unwavering ability to embrace light. I am so happy whenever our paths cross. To Stephen Shagnahan, for many years of dinners and deep conversations. I can't imagine my life without you in it.

And a very special thank you to my son, Gabriel Erwin, for showing me what I didn't even know was missing. You taught me how to open my heart. I love you more than words can express.

To those I haven't mentioned, you are not forgotten. You've helped me realize and accept that everything I need has been inside me all along. Thank you for your insight and compassion.

Final Thoughts

When you do the work to know yourself, you no longer need the protection of a false outer shell. There is no reason to conceal any part of what makes up who you are because you stand comfortably in your own truth without excuses or hidden judgements. Your inner toolbox possesses everything you need to love and value every single part of you. Honesty, patience, and acceptance of your whole self compassionately guides your way to a balanced and fulfilling life. Making peace with your ego opens possibilities, opportunities, and abundance because you've consciously repatterned your blueprint to believe that you deserve it. Everything you've encountered along the way to get here has brought you closer to recognizing your authentic self. Your journey is a lifelong adventure full of twists and turns that continues to offer insight and growth. No one can tell you who you are or who to be when you discover and accept yourself. Step into your brave new world with love and excitement. It's time to reclaim what is most precious and wonderful. You.

BIO

The Long and Winding Road . . .

I started my career as a clothing designer and morphed into a personal wardrobe stylist after selling my business and having a child. Over the years, I began to discover a unifying theme among my clients. The most necessary cleaning out is in one's internal closet, where memories and experiences are stored, hidden, or displayed. How you present yourself to the world is a reflection of your self-esteem. If you want to be loved, you must first accept and love every part of you. I use my intuitive skills to uncover limiting beliefs, blockages, and the reasons why people feel overwhelmed and stressed. Re-examining and discarding what no longer serves you both internally and externally lets in the happiness you deserve. Learning to connect with yourself is the key to connecting with others and enjoying a fulfilling life. Finding your true self happens when you stop looking. Your inner toolbox possesses everything you need to learn to love and value every single part of you. Releasing the pain that has held you back from embracing a balanced and fulfilling life opens new possibilities and opportunities. You have no idea how much abundance is waiting for you until you repattern your blueprint to believe that you deserve it.

Author's Note

About the Author
Pier Pagano holds an MFA in Creative Writing and English from the City University of New York, along with certifications in mindfulness and related studies. She is an international wellness consultant and has been featured on podcasts as the creator of the Repattern program. She spends her time between Los Angeles and NYC. This is her first book.

For more information about Pier and her blogs visit www.lifeessencetribe.com

About the Editor/Curator
Stacy Higgins is the editor and curator for *No One Can Tell You Who You Are Except You*. Stacy is a designer and manager of several websites for artists and educators. She is a trained jeweler and has owned and operated home furnishing retail stores for over 20 years in LA and NY, along with writing monthly home trend columns in several Style magazines. Stacy resides with her husband in beautiful St. Petersburg, Fl. stacy@lifeessencetribe.com.